A VOYAGE
FROM KASHMIR...
(MERI ZINDAGI KA SAFAR NAMA)

Abdul Rehman Khan – 1970s

Abdul Rehman Khan, as told to
Aamnah Rahman

authorHOUSE®

AuthorHouse™ UK
1663 Liberty Drive
Bloomington, IN 47403 USA
www.authorhouse.co.uk
Phone: UK TFN: 0800 0148641 (Toll Free inside the UK)
        UK Local: 02036 956322 (+44 20 3695 6322 from outside the UK)

Published by AuthorHouse 08/07/2020

ISBN: 978-1-7283-5553-5 (sc)
ISBN: 978-1-7283-5554-2 (hc)
ISBN: 978-1-7283-5552-8 (e)

Print information available on the last page.

This book is printed on acid-free paper.

In the loving memory of my mum and dad

CONTENTS

FOREWORD

This is a summary of my father's life story as well as a reflection (part his and part mine) on some of the events that occurred in his life. My father was not a *hero* by any means, just an ordinary man who had some influential experiences that I felt needed to be shared with others.

I have often felt, like so many others that the contributions of soldiers from the Indian Sub-Continent and other parts of The Common Wealth (countries that were part of the British Empire) have not been acknowledged and given due respect, which has caused sadness as their efforts and sacrifices have gone unrecognised. The Servicemen and women from the Common Wealth countries who fought in World War I and World War II made substantial contributions to the Allied Forces.

Hence, one of my reasons to write about my father's time in the army. First, he served in the British Indian Army and after the partition of India and Pakistan took place, he was appointed in the Pakistani Army. This book is not a comprehensive account of all his time spent in the army, as he did not openly speak about his time in service – maybe it was too painful to voice. Also, a section of a book relaying one man's story will not do justice to the greater cause and nor will it give a complete account of what life was like during the war years, but I hope it sheds some light on certain key occurrences.

I also want to highlight to future generations of young people whose origins are from the commonwealth countries to know that their ancestors played a part in shaping history. The freedom and privileges we have today are a result of the sacrifices made by the previous generations.

My father's childhood ended abruptly, at the young age of twelve due to the death of his father. He had to learn to be strong and so, he had developed some of his fighter spirits before joining the army. As an almost, seventeen-year-old boy without a proper birth certificate at the time, the army shaped the rest of his conditioning, he had to learn life skills rapidly and become a man to survive. Some parts of the book—like my father's early years and his journey to England will hopefully reflect the norms of society particular to that time. This is a historical recount through a personal narrative of an ordinary person's experiences and perspectives.

Other reasons for me to write about parts of my parent's life have been to demonstrate the struggles that people of their generation faced when they first arrived in the United Kingdom (UK) in the 1950s and 1960s. The first generations that came here to the UK did not only come here for themselves; they came here to improve the quality of lives of the families and loved ones they left behind too. They struggled for many years leading difficult and impoverished lifestyles to make life better for their families. In some cases, the families that were left behind in their motherland had a better quality of life and lifestyle due to the money that was sent from the UK to fund beyond their necessities. As families in the UK would live on the bread line to ensure, the loved ones left behind were comfortable beyond what they would normally be able to afford.

Whilst this book is based upon my father's life, the other person who impacted our lives greatly was our mother. She was an incredibly strong-minded, genuine, and caring individual who had to cope with many hardships. She was probably the strongest influence upon my brother and me. She was not an educated woman, compared to the modern-day perspective; she had a basic schooling from Pakistan and could read Urdu. My mother had a strong faith and high moral values, which together with her resilience helped her to overcome great difficulties.

Sadly both my parents have passed away but their memories live on in our hearts and minds, especially our mothers. I wanted this to be a tribute to them both and a legacy for future generations of my family to take forward, to learn and understand their history.

I collected the notes over a while in various ways; some were stories that my parents shared with us as children and some were more specific notes that I made (particularly the years of my father's army life) whilst speaking to him in the last few years of his life. I had started the writing in 2003 but left it for years before I finally picked up the notepad and started to word process the first draft of the notes I made whilst my parents were alive. I could not motivate myself to write earlier as I found the memories painful so I kept delaying it. But then if I had done so, I would not have been able to capture the remaining part of my father's life. I regret not doing this earlier and maybe at least my father could have seen the finished version—he probably would want me to make edits for some parts.

Aamnah Rahman

CHAPTER 1

ON THE DAY

It is about 11.00 a.m. on Tuesday, 10 June 2003. I cannot be sure as the clock is inside the house, but it feels so—if it was later, the heat of noon would make itself felt. I have been here in Azad Kashmir (Pakistan-administered Kashmir) for about two months. I am sitting on the veranda at home. My wife and daughter are here with me, and my son and his family are in England.

Today is not particularly hot, as you might expect it to be in June in this part of the world, but the sun is beating down through the clouds. It has been cloudy for the best part of four days, with hot winds that are a blessing, as they bring a slight break from the humidity of the summer sun. The clouds have broken the heatwave of the last ten days or so, but it is still very hot. The only problem with these winds is that the dust flies and covers everything— and it has not rained for more than a month.

My elders used to say that the winds come at around this time of year for four days as it is the time of the annual *jaloos* (remembrance) of *Pir Neheri*, a saint buried in what we call *Muqabzah Kashmir*—occupied Kashmir or India-administered Kashmir. I am not quite sure what the *jaloos* is for but I presume it marks an anniversary, either birth or death, which is a common practice in South Asia concerning Sufi saints. People gather at the saint's shrine at a certain point in the year.

My wife, Ghulam Saeeda Begum, known as Saeeda and I are now both pensioners and had longed to return home, to spend time at our ancestral birthplace, to live in our house, and to be with our brothers and sisters, of those who are still alive. I have spent over forty years in the United Kingdom but have returned here several times for short holidays. When I came over in 1971 and 1999 for extended visits, my family was here too, and we stayed in our own house. I had not planned to come back this time, but my wife came over in February and then rang a few days after she arrived to give me some sad news: my only sister had a serious, life-threatening illness. She thought I should be here at this time, so I came as soon as I could. Thanks to Allah the Almighty, my sister is still alive and her treatment is ongoing.

We miss our son and our grandchildren and it is very hot, but we also like it here in the village because of the much quieter pace of life, relatives and friends all being nearby. We enjoy spending time in the house with its open courtyards, and of course the sun. People start to come early at around 7.30 a.m. and they come and go during the day. Everyone comes by—my brother, my wife's sisters, our cousins, all our nieces and nephews, the neighbours ... it is an open house. Our children are not used to this environment; they would say that we are a shared entity and would feel uneasy with the lack of privacy, as people come and go all the time. We have always had an open house in England too, just like most Kashmiri or Pakistani homes of our generation where people did not give the notice to come and visit—they were welcome to come round any time. But usually, people would not come first thing in the morning or hang around until late at night unless they were close friends, neighbours, or relatives visiting from a distance or staying over.

This is the third time we have had our house built and resurrected since we got married in 1954. Although this house was only completed in 1998, just over four years ago at the time I am writing of, we have had more work done to the house again. Each time we come, something has gone wrong or stopped working, so it always requires some sort of maintenance work. This time the doors and windows needed to be varnished due to the damage caused by the hot sun. It is not like England, where we have PVC doors and windows, so we do not have to bother with painting anymore. I remember when we did have wooden doors and window frames, but even then it was something you did once in a decade or so.

I should give the credit to my wife for having all this work done, as my health does not allow me to stand and supervise the work in this heat. The last two times we had this house resurrected and built again, she was here to oversee it all and provide the catering for the workmen. In 1971–1972, when the second version of the house was being built, she had two very small children to look after too. Then she came over in early 1997 and stayed for almost two years while the current house was built. Her health suffered, but she persevered and waited until it was all completed.

It is a very different house to the previous one, which was small and consisted of three rooms, a washroom, and the courtyard, which was just a natural ground, part clay and part grass, not chipped as it is now. By today's standards, it was a basic house, but back then, because it was new and built out of bricks, it was called a '*pakha makaan*', meaning 'solid house.'

When I purchased this land to build our house in the mid-1950s, it was almost out in the open countryside, but now as the village has expanded; it is surrounded by housing on all four sides. The large house we have today has two entrances on both floors, but only the downstairs has access to the garden and the narrow street outside. The first floor leads onto a large veranda on three sides of the house, which offers views of the village on three sides and looks across the fields on the other side. The ground-floor entrances also lead to verandas which adjoin the courtyard, which is partially paved with chipped patterns, a common design here. The original water well is still in the garden at the end of the courtyard but is now covered with a metal grid. There used to be a square raised platform round the side of the well, but that has been dismantled, and now the surface of the well is at the same level as the garden.

So as I sit here on the veranda of my house, I have reflected on my life and pondered in the past and what was it all for? I ask myself if it was worth it or should I have stayed here in the village like so many others and try to carve a future for myself? Would my family (wife and children) have been treated well and would they be talented to make something of themselves or would they have been misguided into chaos and feudalism like some of my nephews and nieces were? How my destiny and fate guided me from a boy in this village to lands far away and back? Lots of questions enter my mind; I am now elderly and matured; I have lots of time to reflect and ponder.

This is 'meri zindagi ka safar nama', the story of my life's voyage from Kashmir...

In the garden, Channi Kanjal

CHAPTER 2

THE VILLAGE OF PANJERI

Panjeri, my home village, is a Chib Rajput settlement. The people here claim to be direct descendants of Maharajah Dharam Chand Rajput Aka Shadab Khan, who was one of the first Hindu princes to convert to Islam in the reign of Babur, a Mughal emperor. He is popularly known as Baba Shadi Shaheed. His shrine is located in the foothills of Bhimber, about fifteen miles from Panjeri. As children, we were told that Shadab Khan descended from Chib Rajput's from the district of Kangra, Himachal Pradesh, India. The other lineage that the *Panjerials* (people of Panjeri) claim to have is that of Maharajah Porus Kshatriya, king of Chenab state, Jhelum River region around 340 AD, who was known for his bravery in defeating Alexander the Great.

The settlement of Panjeri has existed for five hundred years or more. It has had a school for a few hundred years, and traditionally the men have served in the armed services. The people of Panjeri are not typical of rural villagers in this part of the world as they are generally well-educated and advanced in terms of mentality and living standards. This will be hard to believe for people who are not familiar with the *Panjerials* especially those who have set views of people from rural backgrounds. In this part of the world, people from urban backgrounds mainly view people from rural backgrounds as illiterate and backward. You would have to see for yourself to understand what I am referring to: there are doctors, army officers, engineers, teachers, and other accomplished people to be found here en masse. Education has been an important part of life here; the old school was where local children and those from surrounding villages were taught. Whilst the men have been schooled here for decades, my wife's generation were the first females, in the 1940s that went to formal school. Some of my older cousins and village women could read and write in Urdu, and of course, they were taught to read the Quran and given an Islamic education at home by local Islamic tutors, *Maulanas* or *Maulwis*. Later generations of girls went to study the Quran and receive an Islamic education in the mosque madrasa and the national curriculum was taught at school.

*My wife's paternal uncle, Raja Waliayat
Ali Khan, at home in the 1940s*

The Panjerials are proud of their Rajput heritage and so traditionally only married Rajput women. However, a lack of females within the village and their clan led them to seek brides from other Rajput villages in the Punjab districts of Jhelum, Gujarat, and Kharian and other parts of Azad Kashmir. So they are well connected to other clans in the region. When a woman came from a distance to marry a local man, she was often accompanied by a younger brother, cousin, or nephew who acted as a trustee and messenger between her and her birth family. These boys were schooled here too; in the UK, I have come across many who had been to school in Panjeri. The boys went back to their birth families when they became older.

By that time the sister or aunty they had accompanied would have had her children who could act as messengers if needed.

Society in South Asia is still very much governed by the caste and class system. Unfortunately, this is a by-product of a feudal and colonial system here in South East Asia and reflects how certain elements of society still operate. Those with power and wealth control and exploit the vulnerabilities of those who are poor and destitute. They use their power and wealth to influence those less fortunate than themselves and keep them at their beck and call.

Alhamdulillah (thanks to god), fortunately these people are few and far between a lot of good people. However, Panjeri is not an acceptation to this either. There are certain elements of those feudal and politically motivated here too. The people involved choose to use their position in society create chaos, exploit and use people for their own means. In observation of some of these individuals and how think and operate. It has come become apparent that although in appearance they seem to have everything, in reality, they are simply empty-hearted and motivated by greed and the status quo. They can be cunningly sly and will try at every opportunity to take advantage or backstab you. They spend so much of their energies in trying to keep up the appearances that they have lost track and fallen off the path of humanity. It may a little harsh but that is my assessment of them.

Panjeri has become a very different place to the village I left behind over 40 years ago. The enhancement in material wealth and the endeavours of people to seek a better life have had an impact. Sadly, it seems people have changed and become more self-centred. As people are generally affluent, they can afford to be independent and do things for themselves whereas in the past they were interdependent upon each other. Affluence can give rise to self-centeredness, subdued arrogance, rivalry, and lack of kinship. I have seen and felt this selfishness and greed creep into my family too.

On a more positive note, advancement in society and wealth means a significant number of people in this village have all the amenities you would expect to find in a city such as running water, electricity, gas, telephones, computers, satellite dishes, mobile phones, electrical heaters, air-conditioning, and the internet and so on. It is almost the same as England but here in Pakistan only the wealthy have all the amenities that, perhaps we take for granted. I would say that for a rural community, the people of Panjeri are well advanced and generally upper-middle class. Their ways of thinking and standards of living reflect this. However, there are a small number of people whose lifestyle will reflect what you may expect to see in a northern Kashmiri or Pakistani village. These people survive on the income they have at their dispersal and skilfully make ends meet. They are not shy or backward in their thinking, though – they just do not have the means to afford forwardness.

Many people from the Panjeri area still serve in the armed forces in Pakistan. These days a few of our women have taken up the challenge too and are serving alongside the men. In the past, they aimed to become doctors, college lecturers and school teachers as they were the desired professions due to being seen as *izatdar* (respectable) and the reverence that society here places upon them. The changes in cultural thinking and time have enabled the girls, who are excelling the boys in education to broaden their horizons.

There is a degree college for women in Panjeri even though it is still a village. It was an intermediate college (high school) before this. The boy's school is still an intermediate college. The women's college was given preference over the boy's intermediate college to upgrade to a degree college. A college for girls in the village has enabled most of them to attend along with other girls from surrounding villages. In the past, only those who could afford to send their daughters to boarding colleges did so.

In a conservative country such as Pakistan; it is more

difficult for girls from rural backgrounds to go to the cities for education. Even if they can afford to attend, they cannot travel freely without a guardian. It has relieved further pressures on the parents as they do not have to arrange transport for their daughters as they would do when the girls attended colleges in the cities. Panjeri is an affluent place so many households own cars and so some of the girls have learned to drive. Educated and independent women will be the future of our society and hopefully, they will have a good impact on future generations.

Although I am proud of my heritage, I do not wish to be intentionally boastful. Being a good Muslim and human being is more important to me. I believe a person's traits show up in their dealings with people. People will recognise you for whom you are and not what you portray to be.

Chapter 3

BRETHREN AND KINSHIP

I left home at round sixteen and a half years but my heart has remained true to my roots. I have tried to uphold the values of brethren and kinship, even for relatives that live distantly. Being a simple and traditional man, I have always believed in doing what I can for the extended family and do not want anything in return from them. I like so many others of my generation left our homeland to build better a future not just for ourselves but also for those loved ones who we left behind. I just wanted to improve things for all of us so that we could have a better life.

People of my generation who emigrated in the 1950s and 1960s have clung on to their values, thinking, and ways of life. In contrast, the people in Pakistan and other parts of the Indian Sub-Continent have moved on with the time and the subsequent changes in acquired wealth. I cannot quite figure out why things changed the way they did but they did, it is a stark reality for most people. So those who we left behind have moved on with the signs of the times. It seems they have become somewhat indifferent to us in their ways of thinking and some of their values. I suppose that is up to them, and all we can do is hope and pray that Allah SWT will guide us all. It can because of hurt and distress to us all if we let it but not so when we look at the bigger picture – there is more to life than this.

My generation left our homeland with pure hearts, and maybe it was naive but we thought our good intentions and all that we did for the family back home would be at least reciprocated in appreciation and affection. But disappointingly much of what some people have received in return has been envied resentment, mistreatment coupled with misuse of their trust, income, and wealth.

Due to this many people who live abroad are disgruntled with their extended families in the mother country. They have experienced issues such as their property or land being taken from them, misspending of the income that they sent back, and the lack of account given as to how and where it was spent, their families have not been given their rightful inheritance and so on. This is not uncommon in the South Asian communities; I have come across so many people who have experienced similar treatment. The worst part is when the children or grandchildren often get dragged into this to cart people over to Europe and North America through marriage. I'm not trying to be deliberately provocative but whilst the initial intention may be good to join families together through marriage. Often the hidden criteria are usually so that the offspring of people in the countries of origin can go abroad and have a better life for themselves and the family back home.

If we cannot meet their demands, then we become the outcasts of the family which is regretful. We have become the family members who do not have a place in their hearts or kinship structure. I have heard people in England many times state things like that the people back home behave like they do not know us or will only greet you if you go to them – which is sad and disheartening.

Living in the UK, our younger generations have sometimes been caught in the middle of it all. Whilst, on the one hand, they have endeavoured to establish their British identity along with their cultural values, which are marginally different from those of our generation. They have witnessed and observed the treatment that their parents and grandparents have been dealt with by those extended family members in the country of their origin. This is often coupled with the experience of feelings of rejection and 'otherness' (especially if they choose not to tow in line with the status quo) when they visit the country of their ancestors due to some experiences of animosity towards them. They are labelled quite quickly and often it is due to perceptions about them rather than reality.

Habitually, people in our countries of origin seem to consider the younger generations who have been born and brought up abroad as 'simpletons' who do not quite comprehend anything. They often give straight forward answers when being inquisitively interrogated by family members back home or they stay quiet. On the contrary, these youngsters understand almost everything; they are observant and know who is pulling the strings. The reason they respond openly and honestly is because that is what they are used to; they are not familiar with telling lies or not being straight with people. They remain quieted not because they do not understand but more likely as they do not wish to get embroiled with cultural politics and the emotional blackmail that sometimes accompanies it. Besides, they do not want to be seen as disrespectful. The youngsters do vent their frustrations at their treatment when they come back home to the UK, often its arguments with the parents for taking them there!

I suppose there are inevitably two sides to a coin, so those who remained behind have their own opinions on their version of the predicament. Some of them think that those of us who emigrated only think of ourselves and do not have time or care for them. At times they consider the ones living abroad as old fashioned and backward – stuck in their ways. Maybe it so – and it is unreasonable for us to expect people to remain the same as ourselves.

In some cases, people in the Sub-Continent envision the younger generations from their communities who live in the West as being too westernised and not having enough cultural values. At other times they can be brusque and make statements like so what if your forefathers went abroad? What did they achieve for us, and what are they to us? And so on...

Some of them even complain and pronounce that those of us who visit the country of their forefathers from abroad come to flaunt our wealth. Perhaps this is true and some people may be guilty of this. However, what they do not realise or appreciate is how the majority of us have to struggle to scrimp and save this money for these holidays. Besides this, every slight bit of money that visitors and tourists spend in places they visit aids their economy. Consequently, when people construct houses, stay in hotels, eat in restaurants, buy from the shops, and visit points of interest, lease cars or hire taxis, and so on—it all contributes to their economy. It retains people in jobs and generates income for the local community. The economic contribution from those living abroad to countries of their origin is still huge.

Those of who left our homeland are aware of the way things have changed here but sometimes you have to let things go, in our language they call it '*darghuzar karna.*' I also believe in my cultural beliefs where we have a proverb which states that if you lift your *kameez* (shirt), you will merely expose your own naked stomach. Loosely translated it means if you lift the cover on your family affairs, it is like exposing your inner private matters. In our culture, it is sometimes considered as *baistey* (shameful) and weak to allow others to know of your family's inner affairs. Accordingly people are cautious about what they say even though it can be a source of significant distress and pain to them. That is why people of my generation ignored much of what has gone on. Regrettably, some people did not regard it that way and took advantage of things in any way they could. In situations like this, the ancient saying about being able to select your friends but not your family is markedly apt.

In the UK I have sat and listened to the older men speak about it at the Masjid, it is the same story everywhere. Some people are deeply hurt and speak about it openly to the point where they want everyone to know whereas others still do not open up about family business; maybe due to hurt, anger, or embarrassment. They either try playing things down and make-believe that everything is fine or they see opening up to others as a weakness. They are ashamed to admit this has happened and so keep quiet. This is understandable as it is in our culture it is still common to maintain family business private and permit things to be.

In summary, I feel my generation and subsequent generations left our homeland to build better lives for our families and extended networks. Whether or not those who we left behind acknowledge and appreciate it, we have done a lot for these people. Having said all this, it was not always like this. In the initial years, people of my generation were appreciated by our loved ones back home. The efforts we made to better ourselves and their lives had a great impact. There are still a lot of good and very close families. They have not fallen into this degenerating spiral of self-centred conceit and rivalry. It is important to recognise that people in the Indian Sub-continent are part of developing nations and so have naturally moved on with the changes in living conditions and environments. So whilst it may seem to us that they have moved on and left us behind in some aspects, it is not always what it seems on the surface. Many people have not overlooked the importance of blood ties and kinship. Therefore, it is unfair to tarnish everyone with the same brush.

In my religion, we cherish a belief that you do things for the sake of Allah and not for reward from people, so maybe it is best that way. I am a believer and confident our good intentions and deeds will not be wasted. It is possible the reward was not meant for this world but the hereafter, after all, there is a god up there. We will all have to face him on judgement day, therefore let's leave this up to the almighty.

I am pleased that things have changed for the younger generations, and I do not blame them for not seeing the extended family back home as a priority. It is possible, this will mean that they can cultivate a more decent future for themselves instead of being torn apart by two cultures and the status quo as my generation was. I say this not out of any antagonism or malice but hopefully to inform upcoming generations including my grandchildren that they have options available to them. I hope that they do not fall into the same trap as the older generations and become entangled in the cultural and emotional blackmail fuelled by feudalism and greed. I know the younger generations both in the UK and Pakistan are much more savvy and smart – I have observed them. Hopefully, they will be able to come to a consensus on how to take the ties of brethren and kinship forward without conditions.

If we do not learn from this, it will be our combined loss for future generations. It will have far-reaching impacts. Ultimately those youngsters living in the west will almost certainly disassociate themselves from the country of origin of their forefathers. It will be regretful if this happens and they lose contact with blood relatives. This will be accompanied by the lack of dividends that are still sent by those living abroad.

All being well, the youngsters of today will identify who they are and can work out what is better for them. I also hope that they will be appreciative of their heritage and carry that with them as that is what makes them who they are.

CHAPTER 4

MY EARLY LIFE

I am Abdul Rehman Khan Son of Raja Gulzar Khan. I was born around the 10 January 1925 (no official birth certificate), in Panjeri, Distt. Bhimber, Jammu and Kashmir. I was one of five brothers, two of whom died. Jamshed was the eldest; he was two years old when he died. I did not know him as I was the third eldest of my brothers. My older brother Fazal-Ur-Rehman was about seven years older than me, my younger brothers Mohammad Sharif and Mohammad Sarwar were three and seven years younger than me.

I was a bit feisty and naughty as a child. I did not like being told what to do or bossed around which is a trait that I possessed throughout my life. One day my older brother Fazul-Ur-Rehman spanked me for something that I did wrong. I waited until he was bending over trying to tighten the strings on the *manjee* (cot to sit on). Then I picked up a *sanga* (a large wooden fork-like instrument used to gather hay) and struck him in the back and said:

> '*hun sanao – kiskey mara si ah*' (now
> tell me, who did you hit).

Then I ran away from him and he was just left holding his back and shouting in pain '*oh my back ...*'

My older brother Fazal-Ur-Rehman

I was also a joker and would lead the crowd on too but my loyalties were in the right place. Once in a school *Kabaddi* (wrestling) match, which one of the schoolmasters

23

(teacher) was a referee, then one of the other boys hit my second cousin and future brother-in-law, Abdul Qayyum. When I saw Abdul Qayyum was hurt, I did not like it and got annoyed. I then struck the other boy hard; I think I made his nose bleed. The referee turned on me as if to say what you have done; then gave us all a scolding. We felt we had been not heard out; the referee seemed to take the side of the other boys. So out of frustration my cousins and I ended up throwing blocks of clay at the schoolmaster from behind after the match when he was walking home. He did not see which one of us had thrown the blocks of clay but we knew he would go and speak to our *ajji* (older paternal uncle) Raja Farman Ali. We knew *ajji* would be annoyed and he would give us such a telling off. So on the way home, we hatched up a plan to put forward a cousin, Abdul Hamid. He would say that the other boys set upon him and we joined in to fight back. We even rubbed bits of clay and dust on Hamid's face and clothes to make it look like he had been in a fight. We knew that *ajji* would not say anything to Hamid as he was a little younger than us and was very dear to him. If *ajji* found out that it was one of us older ones that had caused the mischief, we would be in for it. Our plan seemed to work but I think *ajji* did know what had happened but he did not say anything. The following day we had the same master for *geographia* (geography), none of us wanted to go into class fearing the consequences of the actions of the previous day but we did. Surprisingly, he did not say anything to us, probably out of embarrassment.

Similar to other Rajput settlements, our village was on high ground and so there was only one single water well that supplied the whole village. It is still there today, a very deep well. It took several months to construct. In our religion and culture, it is *barakah* (blessing) to eat from one plate or drink from one water vessel. This means that eating and drinking together is like 'sharing is caring' – it promotes care and consideration. This well was a blessing and we all shared the water at the time. The well was situated just outside the village on the lower grounds, so men known as *mashqis* (water carriers) used to supply each house with water in clay pot pitchers known are as a *gharra*. The *mashqis* would knock on the outside door known as *davedi* of the courtyard and the women of the house would take the water from there into the house. They would place the water pitchers on a *thallah*, a place in the courtyard where the pots of water were kept.

Whilst, the men took care of everything outside the house such as working in farming the land, growing the crops, feeding the cattle, collecting firewood, buying the rations that we needed, and so on. The women took care of everything in the house which is a huge task anyhow; they ground the flour on hand-operated stone grinders known as a *chakki*, they cooked, cleaned, washed and mended the clothes. They learned skills like weaving clothes on the hand styled looms known as a *charkah*, they learned embroidery and knitting. Many of them prepared items for their dowry from a young age. They also made sweets by hand like *meti roti* (sweets chapatti), *tikkian* (diced sweets made out of flour, milk, ghee, sugar etc), *panjiri* (a dried dessert made out of Rava flour with nuts, etc.), and hand-rolled *seviyan* (vermicelli noodles) and at times of special occasions, they made *metay ladoos* (traditional sweet *samosas filled with semolina, sugar, ghee, aniseed, etc.*). The generation before my wife was taught the Quran, Islamic education, and Urdu at home by local Maulanas or Maulvis (Islamic Tutors).

By the 1930s we had expanded as a village and the water supply was getting scarce as they were now more than a few hundred households. The people of Panjeri owned land all around the village for at least a couple of miles and some land which was a distance from the village. So my father and his cousins including my future father-in-law decided to move out of the original village and build their houses on land that was lower down on plane fields. It was only about one and a half miles away from the original village; this new hamlet was named Channi Kanjal. Many others did the same, so the village of Panjeri became surrounded by little hamlets called *channi* plus one other name all around. The people were all from one lineage and they were still a very close-knit community.

My childhood ended abruptly at the age of twelve as my father died. I was very attached to my father and I loved him very much. My world was shattered and it felt like we were abandoned. We would now be called *yateem* (orphan) and be looked upon in pity. I was in grade five at school at the time of his death and had to leave school to take care of my family duties. My elder brother was away serving in the army and my younger brothers were too small to take on the tasks. My mother was young, in her thirties, and came from a distant village so she had no blood relations nearby. Besides, I came from a Rajput family and in those days the women of Panjeri did not do any tasks out of the house.

I learned to plant and harvest the crops from the land that my father owned, graze the cattle, and collect wood from the local woods known as the *pabhi*. I learned to chop the wood into logs for the fire used for cooking and heating in winters. It was a huge responsibility for a boy of my age, but I feel I was a born fighter. I just got on with it and besides what else could I do? Although, my childhood had been wrecked; I still had self-respect and pride. I could not allow my mother or my unmarried sister who was about four years older than me to do tasks such as this. I had decided to stop being a child and act up to fulfil my duties as a son and brother.

My paternal uncles were busy looking after their own families so they could not take on our upbringing and care too. We all lived next door to each other, our courtyards had little passages to each other's houses and so they were around if we needed any help. Times were good then, money was scarce and people were mainly poor. However, they genuinely cared and looked out for each other. I too had great affection for my uncles and cousin brothers and sisters.

My favourite brother was Mohammad Sarwar, who died aged seventeen in 1948 whilst trying to reach safety. My family like so many others fled their homes on the foothills of Kashmir, bordering what is now Pakistan to escape the Dogra and Sikh *dacoits* (looters) as they were referred to. Sarwar's death was a big blow to me; my favourite little brother was gone and I did not get a chance to say goodbye properly. He was buried in my mother's home village of *Baisa*, Kharian district which is where they had fled in fear of persecution. I was told that as soon as the rumour had spread that the Dogra's and Sikhs were coming; a lot of people just gathered whatever belongings they could and left the village. They all headed towards the village fields that overlooked the water, the other side of the water was now Pakistan. I do not think the *dacoits* came to our part but everything had been prepared for an encounter, the riffles had been checked and loaded. My future in-laws' house was the highest place in our village of *Channi Kanjal* so that is where the ammunition was being stored.

My future sister-in-law, Ruqiah did not want to leave home; she was about 11 years of age then. She wanted to stay behind with her *ajji* (father's older brother) so she was taught how to fire a rifle gun in case she needed to use it. I am not sure if she actually did go across the water with her family or stayed behind with the men. The journey for my future wife's family was not that difficult as their paternal grandmother had come from Pind Aziz, a village just on the other side of the water. It was only a few miles away, so that is where they stayed. My mother's village was about fifteen miles or so away but others had even longer journeys to reach safety.

If I had been around, I would have stayed behind and tried to protect them all. Most of the grown men of the village were serving in the armed forces at the time or working away from home. The only ones left behind were the women, the elderly, and the very young who were defenceless so they had to flee their homes at that time. I am certain that this fear was felt by other communities who feared persecution from the Muslims in other parts of the Indian subcontinent.

My army unit was returning to Lucknow in India when news of the troubles broke out about partition. I did not know what to make of it at the time. I was familiar with *Allama* Mohammad Iqbal's philosophy and *The Quaid*, Mohammad Ali Jinnah's vision of a separate Muslim homeland for the Muslims of *Hindustan* (India) but I was a serving soldier of the British Indian Army. Besides, my home was Jammu and Kashmir which was an independent princely state, and naively I did not think we would be affected by partition.

Just like his forefathers, Hari Singh, our Maharajah was not the kindest of rulers but we, the Panjerials fostered an amicable working relationship with him. Many men from my village served in his cavalry. Even though the maharajah retained this type of relationship and banter with us, the Dogra maharajahs were suspicious people. They were wary of their Muslim Rajput citizens – perhaps they feared an uprising or takeover. I suppose that is what you can expect from those who impose themselves upon others. It made me wonder why they had so many Rajput clans serving in their household staff and cavalry, though. Was it so that they could keep an eye out for rebellion or could it be that the Dogra Raj trusted their Rajput clans more than others so kept them close? There was an underlying trust and belief in *baradari* (clan) and kinship which depicted either a conscious or subconscious part. However, no one would be spared if they dared to go against the maharajah and his rule.

I could tell of many stories of the Dogra Raj's cruelty towards its citizens (Rajputs and other baradaris) that we endured as a people. One of the most prominent atrocities committed by the Dogra raj (rule) to my knowledge at the time was the massacre of twenty-two Kashmiri Muslim men on the 13 July 1931 as they were protesting against the state's prosecution of a Kashmiri freedom fighter who had been charged 'allegedly' with terrorism. They were all killed one by one as they called the *Adhan* (Muslim call to prayer). This day is recognised as *Yaum-e-Shudaha-e-Kashmir* (The Kashmir Martyrs Day) and is marked by Kashmiris on both sides each year.

On a day to day level the people of Jammu and Kashmir, particularly the Muslims endured many hardships under the Dogra totalitarian rule – they controlled almost everything and made life difficult for people. We were not allowed to wear leather shoes or anything made of beef as cow meat and its products were strictly forbidden in Jammu and Kashmir. If cattle died on the other side of the border with Hindustan, we would be able to obtain the leather from there. We would walk around bare footed as we had to wait months to get our shoes mended; the *mochi's* (cobblers – shoe menders) were always busy. Fortunately for us, the border with Hindustan was only on the other side of the water at the end of the village fields

31

but for others, in living further into Jammu and Kashmir it was incredibly difficult.

Hari Singh has several *betakhs* (houses used for sitting/ visits by the Maharajah) in Jammu and Kashmir; we were told that there was one near Panjeri too. He rarely used it; otherwise, we would have heard that he had come to visit.

A man named Allah Ditta Khan from my village joined his cavalry and was on a guard of honour parade; the Maharajah stopped when he reached him and asked him where he was from? When he stated that he was from Panjeri, Hari Singh said '*Ah ben chodh, Panjerial*' (swore at him). Allah Ditta Khan's retorted to this and said '*Tu ben chodh, tera peauh ben chodh*' (you are so and so is your father). Hari Singh had a grin on his face but must have been embarrassed by Allah Ditta Khan's response. Then when one of his close guards shouted '*Mahraj is ney aap ko ghalli dee hai*' (Maharaj, he swore at you). Hari Singh just said '*kio bath nein, apney jaisa hi hai*' (it doesn't matter; he is the same as me).

CHAPTER 5

JOINING THE ARMY

Captain Raja Lal Khan, my maternal uncle.

My older brother was in the 216 Punjab Regiment along with lots of others from my village. I heard about the world war from him and the others.

I travelled by bus from Jhelum to Sialkot to see my *mama ji* (maternal uncle), Captain Raja Lal Khan. I wanted to speak to him about joining the army and to get his permission as he was my elder in my father's absence. I respected my maternal uncles and their judgement; they tried to support my widowed mother in their way. But we were proud people and could not rely on others forever.

I stayed with my uncle and his family in Sialkot for a week; I had never stayed in a city before this. It was very different from the quiet of the village; I came across all sorts of people. It gave time to look around and think things through. My uncle tried to dissuade me from joining, he told me that it was a tough life and besides that, he thought I was too young. He also said, that since my elder brother was already in the army and my younger brothers were too small (though one of them was thirteen now) who would be around for my mother to run her errands and do other chores. I think I heard my uncle and understood his logic but somewhere along the way, I had made up mind to join.

Subedar Raja Bhadar Khan, my younger maternal uncle.

On the way back from Sialkot, I travelled on foot from Saria Allamghir to Panjeri, which is more than twelve miles in distance. I did not have a bicycle at the time, which is what people used as a mode of transport then. I suppose it would be similar to having a motorbike these days. Saria Allamghir is situated on the Grand Trunk (GT) Road which runs through the middle of it, connecting to Jhelum on one side and Lala Musa and Kharian on the other side.

There were other roads from Hindustan known as 'gates or gateways' into Jammu and Kashmir but no real transport unless you found a *tanga* (horse-driven buggy). There was a railway line that British engineers had constructed along the path of the *nehr* (water canal which was constructed around 1910 or just after) which went to Mangla, a garrison town. But I do not think it was used for public transport, just to transport goods.

Before joining I would need my identification documents so a few days later I left home and travelled from Panjeri to Bhimber our local administrative town which is about fifteen miles away to get them. I then travelled from Bhimber to Saria Allamghir, where I boarded a *tanga* to Jhelum which was only a few miles away on the other side of the River Jhelum. There was an old bridge constructed out of steel and iron that connected the two towns, one part of the bridge was a road and the other had the railway line laid on it. The *tanga* drivers and the pedestrians also used the same bridge. I caught the train from Jhelum to Ferozpur. It was the first time on a train and my ticket cost me one rupee. In those days it seemed like a lot of money and people did not travel that much unless they had to.

In the British Indian Army, the White British soldiers were ranked Officers along with *Hindustanis* (Indians) who had attended military cadet colleges as some members of my clan had. The *Dhesi sepoy or sephoy* (traditional/ infantry soldiers) usually progressed as far as the rank of *Subedar* (sergeant). One of my *ajji's* called me 'Subedar' from an early age and that has stuck with me my entire life. In my village men who have military titles or professions are known by that first and then their actual name so you heard *subedar, havaldar, master, doctor sahib, leuftain* (lieutenant), *caphtan* (captain), *carnael* (colonel) and *bargadier* (brigadier) all the time. We even had a General, Fazul Ur Rehman who was from my clan and he was the Prime Minister of Alvar state before partition (all independent Indian states were unified after partition). He died shortly around the time of partition and is buried in Delhi, India. His decedents still live in Saria Allamghir and some of them are in touch with people in Panjeri.

Perhaps the most celebrated soldier of my time from our village was my second cousin Brigadier Raja Habib-Ur-Rehman, who we all called 'Lala Ji' (Punjabi word for big brother). He served with Subhash Chandra Bose

(Netah Ji) in the Indian National Army during the Indian independence struggle from the British. He was even tried for treason to the Imperial King along with three others but they were all pardoned. I do not think there was enough evidence. I was told that the streets of Delhi burst out in celebration upon their acquittal. He was popularly known as '*Fateh Bhimber'* (Conqueror of Bhimber); he had other titles too. He decided to come back to his roots and joined the Pakistan Army after independence. He was a key figure in negotiating with Maharajah Hari Singh at the times of the troubles in Kashmir.

In later years *lala Ji* served as a Military Secretary to Zulfikar Ali Bhutto (Prime Minister and former President of Pakistan). He died in December of 1978 whilst welcoming Zulfikar Ali Bhutto to our village. Bhutto was given a *salaami* (military salute) with a *taup* (barrel gun). The vibration from the gun must have been too much and *lala Ji* collapsed. His death was due to a heart attack. A huge poster picture of him is still situated just outside the boys' college as you enter our village.

*Major Raja Abdul Qayyum Khan – my wife's
eldest brother who also served in the British Indian
Army and then later in the Pakistan Army.*

There were others from my clan and the village that had been gallant as soldiers, one of them had been awarded the Military Cross for his services in the British Army. We used to refer to him as *'lala M.C'* – just meaning 'brother M.C'. Many were keen horse riders including my brothers and they played polo in their army units. Others excelled in other sports such as Lt. Raja Allah Ditta Khan, a pole-vaulter who became respected and famous due to representing Pakistan at the Olympics and Commonwealth Games several times during the 1940s, 50s, and 60s.

CHAPTER 6

ARMY LIFE AND THE WAR YEARS

I was nervous and excited about joining the army. I knew the British liked Rajput soldiers as we were known to be good fighters due to our past. I did not know what to expect; only the things I had heard from others who had served or were still serving in the army. My desire to join was partly to do with family and my *baradari's* (clan's) tradition as that is what we did, we were soldiers. Although my clan had been practising Muslims for several centuries, some of our traditions and values were very much entwined into those of Hindu Rajputs. We dressed and behaved in certain manners, we had certain customs in terms of culture and our dealings with other people and so on. These values were ingrained into us at an early age. My other reason for joining the army was my family's financial status at the time. After my father's death, the only money coming into the household was my elder brother's salary. Even though we lived in a joint family system, he would be getting married shortly so would have a family of his own to support too. So I had to do something to earn money, taking care of the family land and livestock was not enough. I think I had an inclination of wanting to do something so that I could be independent and stand on my own feet too. I had left school due to my father's death; otherwise, I would have gone to complete my matriculation either at Bhimber or Jhelum as that is where most of our people went to study at the time.

Ferozepur was about 145 miles from Jhelum; I travelled there in the summer of 1941 with a man named Abdul Aziz from my village. I saw mile upon mile of the fertile plane fields of the Punjab through the windows of the train. My Kashmir was hilly and mountainous with lush green *wadis* (valleys). My grandfather's *marabah* (land allocated to him for his services to the army) was in Jharanala, Sargodha District. At the time, I had not been there, so this was what it must be like. Abdul Aziz and I arrived at the train station and caught the *tanga* to the cantonment and went to my *Chacha's* (paternal uncle) Raja Ali Akbar Khan's living quarters. My *chacha* was based at the 55 Rissala Depot which was a recruitment centre.

I spoke to my *chacha* about Abdul Aziz and me joining the army and he prepped us a little. The following day or so he took us to see his reporting officer, Major Kennedy who had come to the barracks. He spoke to us; I said to him in Urdu '*Sir, I have come to join*'. He looked at me for a bit and then said '*okay*'. He then sent me to the doctor for a medical. Dr Bassra who examined me was an Indian and spoke in Hindi; he asked me '*how old are you*'? I replied and said '*I am eighteen years of age doctor sahib*'. This was not in line with my Rajput upbringing and values, I did not tell the truth. I was not eighteen; I was barely sixteen and a half years of age. Dr Bassra looked at me, scanning his eyes up and down and then at my uncle. I am not sure if he believed me or not but he did not ask any further questions. Abdul Aziz did not lie, he was sixteen years of age and he told the truth. He did not get recruited but I did. I passed the medical and was accepted to join the same day.

I took our *qasam* (oath) in Urdu/Hindi, it went something like this '*mein qasam katha hoon, key mein is desh ka wafadaar rahoon gha aur jo cheese is kay haq mein ho ghi karoon gha aur jo mukhalif ho ghi who nein karaoon gha ...* '(I take the oath to be faithful to this country and do (defend) whatever is in its betterment and not do anything which is against it ...). I cannot remember the exact words now but I did take an oath of allegiance to the military.

After that, I spent six months in training at various places. It was not all how I had envisaged it to be. During my first few weeks of training in Lucknow, I saw my first horrific scene when we were about to practice our parachute landings from a plane for which we would be paid an extra sixteen rupees per month. A Sikh recruit, who jumped out of the plane just before me, his parachute did not open upon landing! I was due to jump straight behind him; I saw blood and parts of his body scattered all over the ground in front of me! They had to pick all the disintegrated parts of his body and put them in brown sacks. The rest of us did not try landing from a parachute that day. This incident left me horrified and almost paralysed with fright. I felt my stomach sink but I had to continue, there was no going back. I was proud, I could not even bear to think about failure. How would I tolerate the stigma of being known as someone who went for military training but did not pass due to fear? People would say that I was a '*bouzdil*' (coward). That would be a total catastrophe – I would be seen as a '*nalaiq*' (inapt). Besides this, I had wanted to become a soldier so I had to accept that things would go wrong and death would be an inevitable part of this journey. I went onto witness other horrendous and traumatising scenes in the years to come.

I was then sent to my unit in Babina Cantonment, Uttar Pradesh. Babina was a big and busy base, lots of soldiers and I kind of took a liking for it straight away. I saw and met British and Indian soldiers; I had heard much about the '*Engraize*' (English) from my elder cousins and uncles but never actually met anyone of them in person until joining the army.

During six months of military training, I learned how to operate riffles, drive an armoured car and heavy jeep (later I drove a tank), handle rifles and machine guns; I cleaned vehicles, learned Roman Urdu (written in English but spoken in Urdu) which I had to pass to get into the English class. I used to get up at 6:00 am, breakfast consisted of tea and a small *puri like paratha* (buttered chapatti), then physical education was at 7:00 am followed by the other training. Lunch was at noon, usually, *daal* (lentil) and *roti* (chapatti), and supper was around 6:00 pm. I had a routine every day which became part of my life until old age; it was good to have something to get up for each morning. Sunday was a holiday that I spent cleaning the barrack (where I stayed). My wage was sixteen rupees per month, after training they gave me rise to thirty-two rupees per month which increased to eighty rupees per month after I was deployed.

We had fun too. We, the Kashmiri and Hindustani soldiers teased and played pranks on each other. In Allahabad or Illahabad, Gurbachan Singh another recruit would leave a rope on his car as a marker when he cleaned it. We used to move the rope and fasten it to our cars and drive his car around, without realising this he would clean our cars too. Afterwards he would ask:

'Oh thusi sarey kethi si, kone lay ghia sey meri ghadhi' (where were you all, who took my car)? The *Subedar* (Sergeant) would tick us off for doing this but it was all innocent fun.

After six months of training, I was given twenty days' leave to go home. When I reached home, everyone was so happy to see me. My mother who was initially reluctant for me to join the army had changed her mind – she was the first person to greet me. The whole village gathered around, the *manjees* (cots to sit on) in the courtyard were all full. I had taken bananas and grapes home. The fruit was not widely available in all parts of the Indian Subcontinent then; we were only familiar with fruits that grew in our regions. So not many people had seen bananas in the village as they grew in other parts of the country; one of my small nieces took one and asked what it was? Our neighbour *Baba* (fatherly figure) Kala Khan had a bout of diarrhoea; I offered Baba Kala Khan two bananas and he ate them – that made him constipated! He later planted seeds in his *bagh* (garden), so then he had a banana plant of his own.

After returning from leave, I was deployed on the 30 December 1941 to Rissala Number 11 Cavalry at Ferozepur, Punjab, India. My first posting was the seaport of Basra, Iraq. We travelled from Ferozepur to Karachi by train; it took a day and night to reach Karachi. Then from Karachi to Basra through the sea which took more than two days and nights. It was my first time at sea; I was seasick with dizzy spells and sickness. We had hens and other small animals on board too but as we travelled further into the sea, and the waters became choppier. The men started to get more seasick so those who had the hens let them go. The men in my unit were mainly Kashmiris and Punjabi's, Muslims, Hindus, and Sikhs – we spoke our language (Punjabi) amongst ourselves but Urdu/Hindi as our official language.

Basra was an old city, it was cold and the people were all Arabic speaking. We stayed there for two months, camped just outside the city. One night whilst we were asleep, the local Arabs stole some of our tents. In the morning we had to search through the whole village to get them back. We were more alert from then onwards as this could be the start of more to come.

My unit moved around a lot during the war so from Basra we moved to Baghdad and surrounding areas, then later onto Syria and Palestine. From Palestine, we went onto Cairo, Egypt, and then through the desert to Libya. Then we crossed the Mediterranean Sea from Libya to Italy where I became a prisoner of war with others briefly for a short period of about twenty days. The Italians released the Hindustani troops but kept our British officers. The British officers were probably worth more to them as captives than we the Indian troops were. We were sent back to Benghazi, Libya. Later we crossed the Mediterranean Sea again this time from Libya to Turkey.

The Arabs seemed to come across as arrogant and harsh people, not like what I had envisaged them to be. They spoke to us and asked belittling questions such as 'Anta Hindu kaffir' (are you Hindu kafir – Arabic for non-believer of Islam). When those of us who were Muslims recited the Kalimah (Islamic oath to say there is no god but Allah and Muhammad is his messenger) to them, they were taken aback and looked puzzled. Perhaps their attitude towards us was due to their lack of knowledge of other cultures or perceptions of Hindustanis. This was a similar scenario wherever we travelled in the Arab world. In Libya, some of them referred to our Sikh soldiers as 'Haji Baba' (men who had performed the Hajj – the Muslim pilgrimage) because of their turbans and kept saying 'Haji baba marhabah' (welcome haji baba). The Sikh soldiers took their turbans off and jokingly showed off their armpits to show the native Arabs their hair to make them realise they were not Muslim.

Whilst in Egypt we were on high alert as we had heard of the Germans and their General Romal (Rommel). He had a tough reputation and his soldiers were strong soldiers – as we were too. The dessert climate was harsh; it was very hot during the day – even hotter than summers back home. The nights were cooler but the water was scarce and we had to be careful, any wrong move could be very costly. The thing that I found the most difficult to control was my liking for tea. By now I had broken off the wooden bits off from several riffles that I had confiscated from fighting with the Germans and collected from dead German soldiers as part of the task of de-arming the enemy. I burnt the wood part to light as firewood to make tea! The British soldiers introduced us to cigarettes too, they gave them to us for free – smoking a cigarette was calming and helped us to cope. At the time I did not know how damaging it would be to my health as that was what we all did. I did not give up smoking until I was in my eighties.

By now, I had learned to drive a tank. The dessert environment allowed me to have plenty of practice. Each tank had a team of seven, although we had our task, we had to learn all the operating drills and mechanics including operating the gun. I was more suited to driving a tank than being a soldier on foot with a rifle – at least I could not break it! Besides I was not in the front rows of the firing lines, I was further behind so being a tank driver was better. I cannot say that I enjoyed firing directly at the enemy but it is something you had to do on the battlefield; it was either us or them. But consciousness told us that they were humans like us too, scared, and afraid.

They probably had families back home too – mothers, fathers, sisters, brothers, wives, and children. Most of them were probably there for the same reasons as we were, believing what we were doing was the right thing to protect humanity. Unfortunately, this is what happens in conflict people become convinced that the doctrine they have been accustomed to is the only way. I did get shot at a few times but thanks to God I never got hit seriously enough to sustain a major injury or death. I was inflicted with a few scratches and minor shrapnel wounds but that was a common thing for soldiers at war and it was not considered as anything serious. I had accepted death as a reality of war early on in my training but left it to Allah's will. As Muslims, we believe the time of your death and the circumstances are written before your birth so whatever is written in your fate is meant to be.

Misr (Egypt) was the country that was the friendliest out of all the countries that I had travelled to so far in the Arab world. One day in Cairo, Mohammed Sharif who was from my village and I were sat by a fountain in *Zulekha* Square near *Bab'e Yusuf* (the gate of Yusuf). We were speaking in our native dialect of Punjabi and a man who had been hovering around for a bit approached us and asked '*Where are you from back home*'?

We were surprised to find someone here speaking our local dialect. We started talking to him and as it turned out he was also from Panjeri and come here in the First World War. He had not gone back; instead, he had stayed and married a local woman. He invited us back to his house for tea; he had four daughters, they all spoke Urdu and Arabic. He even offered us both a hand in marriage for his daughters. We were a bit taken aback; I was not old enough to be married then and Mohammed Sharif was already engaged to be married upon his return home. We declined his offer and pointed out that we were serving soldiers and could not do this. I think he understood as he had been a soldier himself.

He asked us to take a letter to his family when we returned home but also made us promise him not to let onto his family about his status. He had done well, he had married an only daughter of a wealthy Egyptian family and so was a rich man. We took the letter and promised to hand it to his family upon our return. I do not know what it was in the letter but I hand-delivered to his family some years later when I returned to Panjeri. But sadly, his family back home did not respond positively as they probably thought he would come back and ask for his share of the inheritance (the family land, etc.). If they had responded to his letter, they would be have been better off as he would probably marry his daughters back into the family and they would bring their wealth with them too.

During my brief spell as a prisoner of war, we had the

festival of Eid-Ul-Adha (*Bakra Eid*). We had not eaten anything and it was late afternoon, we asked our captors for food and they brought us what looked like a donkey for our feast! We were shocked by this, as this animal looked like a cross between a donkey and a horse. I later became to know that these animals were mules. Back home to sacrifice a donkey for an Eid feast would be seen as an insult as a donkey (although very hard working) was seen as a bit of a meagre animal. We would normally sacrifice a *maaj* (buffalo like cattle) or *bakra* (a male goat) as the maharajah did not allow us to sacrifice a cow. People in our culture often refer to others as 'donkey' as if to say they are lacking in *akhl* (common sense). We told the Italians that we did not eat this meat; for some reason, their officers seemed to think that Hindustanis ate donkey meat (probably due to ignorance).

I also spent two months in Constantinople (Istanbul) Turkey where my unit was camped on the hills overlooking the Bosporus Straits. We did not enter the main part of the city but stayed camped on the hillside. It was a busy shipping channel even then, and I remember seeing a different culture. Atta Turk's people were mainly Muslim but a bit different from other Muslims. They looked like Europeans and they were more westernised. They dressed in western clothes and their language was written in roman script.

Upon our return route from Constantinople, we travelled by sea to Syria. Then by road through Iraq, Iran, and finally what is now Pakistan back to Rawalpindi. After two months in Rawalpindi, the unit was moved to Allahabad. By now it was 1945 and news had started to circulate that the Germans had started to surrender; this was good news as it meant that war was almost coming to an end.

But just then we were struck with another shock, the Japanese had attacked Burma and had dropped bombs on Calcutta too. They had attacked Hindustan and inevitably we would be dragged into another conflict. The war in Europe had been distant for most people. Only those of us who were involved in the war and our families were impacted directly but this attack was on our home soil and it was very real for everyone. My unit was sent to Manipur and Assam, then onto Rangoon in Burma where I was an ambulance driver, carrying the wounded to the hospital. Conditions were harsh as the supply lines had got cut off several times and the ammunitions and rations stocks were low. We stayed there a few months, some days we even had to boil wild plants for food. I was one of the few who came back to Ahmednagar in India for four weeks to collect more rations and ammunition supplies.

Now as the war in Asia had heightened; we were now heading to Mumbai from where we would travel by sea to Malaysia and enter Kuala Lumper. Here I saw lots of poor people, even poorer than those back home who were begging for food – it saddened my heart. These people were suffering; all we could do is to offer hope. The unit spent two months in Kuala Lumper, before heading further south to cross the sea towards the Indonesian islands of Sumatra and then Java. We stayed some months on both islands and I had learnt some words of Batco (Indonesian language) too.

It was the summer of 1945 the Japanese had been weakened as we heard they were being attacked by the Russians in these regions. So they had started to surrender in some areas, we collected the weapons that they left behind. Then in the first ten days or so of August of that year, we heard that the Americans had dropped the biggest bombs ever made (Atomic bomb) on two Japanese cities and they were flattened! Shock, disbelief, triumph, jubilance, relief soon turned into worry and anguish. What would happen next? Would the Japanese retaliate? Did they have similar bombs and would they use them? If yes, where would they drop them? Thankfully they did not respond and surrendered instead. After this, it was back to Kuala Lumper in Malaysia and then by road onto Thailand, Burma before returning to Sikanderabad, India where I was posted as a storeman.

After Sikanderabad, the whole regiment was sent back

to base in Lucknow to rest for six months. Here I went for further training. I had not been home in over five years as there was not any holiday during the war period. My family only knew that I was alive by the remittance they would receive for each month and the odd letter that I could send back. It was now 1947, after six months in Lucknow I was given two months' leave to go home.

I did not know much about my other cousins and men from my village that had served in the World War as we were in different units and regiments. We had served in different places. Thankfully my brother and cousins were safe and alive. My future wife's family had lost two cousins paternal cousins, both brothers who were serving Africa. My future brother-in-law's unit was passing through Tanzania when he came across their graves, he did not know so it was a great shock to him. Many others had not come back. I was one of the lucky ones who lived to tell the tale.

CHAPTER 7

INDEPENDENCE AND PARTITION

The struggle for independence from the British had started in the early 1930s but the war years had made it more evident – a reality. There was daily news of demonstrations and riots breaking in parts of the Indian Sub-Continent. We were soldiers and had another job to do, unlike the police forces who had to enforce law and order and punish their people at the orders of their masters.

As the struggle for Indian independence intensified, a new uprising had started too, the call for a new Muslim nation of Pakistan. During this time Hindustan had gained its independence from *Britannia* (Britain) and Pakistan was to be created, the process of partition had started. A lot of things had gone wrong in Kashmir too, the Maharajah had taken away artillery from the Muslim forces which led to the invasion of Kashmir by Pakistan backed Afghani tribesmen. Jammu and Kashmir had been ruled by an

Afghan dynasty in the past. Whilst the people were mainly indigenous the rulers had been imposed upon them. The latest ruling family of Jammu and Kashmir had purchased the state from the British only over a hundred or so years ago. During the troubles, Hari Singh reluctantly acceded Jammu and Kashmir to India temporarily but as far as the Muslim majority in the state was concerned this was treachery. He had betrayed us and sold us out to another occupation. So a battle was now being fought for Jammu and Kashmir between India and Pakistan, Hindu, Muslim, and Sikh.

Sadly the Indian Sub-continent had been split into various parts. It was unfortunate that two countries who were previously one country were now enemies. But perhaps the saddest thing was that people who were one nation had been torn apart. We were now varying from each other whereas once we were one community. We had our differences but I suppose you can expect that anywhere. I now belonged to a new country, Pakistan which was created in the name of Islam. Whilst Pakistan probably came out of the partition much worse off economically, financially, and militarily but there was a great spirit amongst the people to build this new nation. Having a Muslim homeland meant we would not be treated as second class citizens in our country as many had experienced this in the past.

In unified India, upper-caste Hindus seemed to dominate most things. They had a better education, jobs, privilege, more wealth, and were generally more prosperous. Although our village was predominantly Muslim, we had some Hindu Brahmin goldsmiths and other tradespeople living in the area. We played with their children but never inside their homes as they used to say *'pittah kar chadiah hi'* (you have made it impure) even if we entered their gardens. That is how they thought of Muslims, similar to the *Dalit's* (lower caste Hindus) as being subhuman and impure. There were Sikh villages just a few miles away and we had interaction with each other. But now, most of the Hindus and Sikhs from our region had gone to India and Muslims from India were fleeing to Pakistan.

Our homeland Jammu and Kashmir has been split into two! Jammu and Kashmir ended up being divided partly controlled by India and Pakistan. Since our part of Kashmir was now under Pakistani control, there was little cause for me to go back to India so I did not go back to Lucknow. Instead, I went to Nowshera cantonment and presented myself there. I was now to be enlisted into Pakistan's army. I was stationed at Rawalpindi for four months and then transferred to Jhelum which was so near to home.

In late 1948 I was sent to Gharri Dupatta Village near Muzaffarabad (Azad Jammu & Kashmir). I had been tasked with a machine gun to fire at Indian areoplanes but none came in the four months I was there. It was a quiet place compared to the other cities I had been stationed in. The war was further ahead in Kashmir; I could see the smoke in the mountains and hear the noise of the guns.

I learned to ride a horse properly during this time and became to be known as a 'sawaar' (rider). Horses were a popular mode of transport for the Pakistani army at the time as they did not have much machinery and artillery.

My last posting was in Kohat, northern Pakistan until 1952. I became ill; I had my first seizures, I had developed Epilepsy. I am not sure if it was due to the war or some other cause but I was given an early discharge from the army on medical grounds. I was now nearly 31 years old, the war, and all that I had seen during had shaped me from an innocent and naive boy barely not even seventeen years of age into the man that I was now. I had experienced the harshness and brutality of war – it had left its mark on me. I would never forget. I had experienced sadness and lost colleagues who were like brothers to me and witnessed enemy soldiers fall too.

I had seen and experienced far more than I could have envisaged thirteen years back. I had travelled to various lands and seen different people and their ways of life. We were defending what we were told were our values – even though I still question and sometimes struggle to see exactly what those values were supposed to be. Were these values native to us or were they imperialistic that had been thrust upon us? We were a people who had been occupied ourselves but we went along with the doctrine which had been carefully pierced into our minds. Likewise, even though what took place was atrocious and beyond humanity, the other side would have been told the same-similar things to us. They were in the right and we were wrong.

Perhaps, we thought our independence would come from this too, which it did. But not without the loss of hundreds of thousands of lives of Hindustani soldiers at war and the civilians that struggled for independence at home. I went from being a Kashmiri soldier serving in the British Indian Army, then a Pakistani soldier to a stage where my future was now uncertain. I had never thought of leaving the military early so had not made any plans for the future. One thing was certain; I would not sit around and feel sorry for myself. Thanks to the Almighty I was alive and had my faculties and limbs so I would make an honest living somehow.

CHAPTER 8

CIVILIAN LIFE AND NEW BEGINNINGS

I had been home for some months, it was now 1953 and I was due to be married to my second cousin (we shared the same paternal great grandfather); she was only nineteen years of age some twelve years younger than me. When I left home to join the army she was only about six or seven years old. I still remember her playing with the other girls in the courtyards but now she had grown up. I was happy that I would be starting a new life; I had done what I could so far for my mother and family. My younger brother Sharif was also serving in the army and my older brother Fazal-Ur-Rehman was now married with children. He had a few years of service left before retirement. I did not have the same pressures of supporting the family anymore but I would seek employment in some kind of industry.

Although poverty was still an issue in the sub-continent

it was also a time of affordability – people did not complain about inflation and prices of things as they do now. Many of the items for our staple diet such as wheat for flour, rice, lentils, and spices were home-grown. The livestock produced the dairy products and meat so we did not need to buy much – we were self-sufficient.

Our marriage ceremony was quite simple by today's standard. People were not materialistic in those days but my father-in-law to be Raja Munshi Anayat Khan was a wealthy man, he had a lot of lands in the village and around the region. The *'Munshi'* title was given to him as he kept records for the village and at his work. He had served as a ranger in Jammu and Kashmir and was an educated man, which is why my brothers-in-law were able to study at boarding colleges in Jhelum and Lahore. My wife to be was the youngest of his three daughters; the other two were also married to my cousins. My wife was given cattle which would be the equivalent of a car in modern times amongst other things in her dowry. Jewellery in those days was mainly in silver but there was gold too, they were much larger pieces than now and it was very heavy. The *Barthans* (crockery) were usually made out clay but the big ornaments and serving dishes were made out of *Tambah* (brass).

After getting married I went to work in security at Karachi Shipyards in 1954, my wife joined me later. I already had lots of extended family working there; so I would not be alone. Karachi was the capital city of Pakistan at that time and it was a vibrant and thriving place. We all settled around Raithey Lane, Lalu Khaith, which was a working-class migrant colony. Many people from other parts of Pakistan and those that had come from India during partition had settled there.

From 1956 onwards my relatives started to call their wives to join them so I invited mine too. She joined me in October 1958. Field Marshall Ayub Khan had just declared Marshall Law so all women were required to wear a *burkha* (veil and outer garment). When I went to pick my wife from the train station, I handed her the '*Afghani Burkha*' (veil with holes in the eye area, the rest is covered) that I had purchased for her to wear. She looked puzzled and the shock showed on her face. She looked at me asked 'what is this'? I told her that all women had to wear this because of Marshal Law. She was used to wearing a *chador* (big scarf) but nothing like this. We did not observe *purdah* (covering of face and body) as such in the village, everyone dressed modestly and the women wore a thick chador in the winter or a dupatta (thinner scarf) in the summer months to cover their hair. She took it and wore but on the way home, she kept saying 'I feel sick and suffocated!

Most of the men and women in our network in Karachi were either our cousins or friends. My wife's best friend from childhood and her husband were there too. We spent some good years in Karachi; we worked during the week and got together on Sundays. We would go to the cinema, the beach or gather at one of the many relatives' houses for meals. Our first child, a son was born there in 1959; sadly he was a stillborn child.

By 1958, news of relatives travelling to England from the village started to arrive by the day; my first cousins had already left to seek new fortunes. We got to see them off before they set off for England as all the international flights at the time were from Karachi, so they came and stayed with us before departing. The flights used to go from Karachi to Germany and then to England. Some of the men had already started to send sponsors to others to come and work in the mills. I was still undecided at the time. I had to think about my health, what would happen if my condition which had been under control for some years got worse there?

It was now 1960 and it would mean sending my wife back to the village to be with the family. I could not take her with me as at the time, it was mostly the men who were going. Taking my family with me would mean having to arrange separate accommodation and incur extra expenses for the travel. That is the main reason why the men went by themselves at the beginning. They had to secure employment and establish themselves before inviting their families over. By the beginning of 1961 many of my relatives who lived here in Karachi had gone to England so in the spring of that year, I moved back to the village with my wife and new-born son, Zafar Iqbal. He was a few months old and was not a well-child. It would be better to be near the family.

The *Sikha* (currency) changed from silver to today's money (around 1961), the old monies were all handed into the banks to exchange it for new money. My sister-in-law's family was very wealthy too; they even had a stash of the old gold and silver money. Unfortunately, they were suspicious and buried their gold and silver coins and jewellery (mainly silver) in pots which were placed in holes that had been dug inside their house. Their house was made of stone but the floors were all plastered with mud, as were the walls and rooftops in those days so they could be dug back up. I informed my elderly auntie of the changes in the *sikha* but she and son out of fear or suspicion denied that they had money to exchange; so it did not get exchanged, their loss I suppose but I did my bit.

Chapter 9

COMING TO ENGLAND

By January 1962, I had made my mind up to go to England too, and so on 30.3.1962, I left Pakistan. Zafar had died a few months earlier aged nine months, my wife was still grieving. My elderly mother was also sad for me and my family; she was also convinced that she and I would not see each other again. I remember her wailing and crying as the whole village came to see me off when I left for England, in those days *waliayat* (abroad) was seen as a distant and far culture and people's return was not near. I did not see my mother alive again; she died in 1964, two years after I came to England. I was in hospital then and was not able to go back to see her.

Unlike most of my other cousins and men from my village, my reasons for coming to England were more do with my health than economics. My epilepsy was under control but the pains in the back were getting worse. Like my cousins and village men, I had planned to stay in England for about two years. They were of thinking of making money and I was hoping that I would get treatment for my back and joints. I did not feel like the British owed me anything but did want better prospects and health; I wanted to return home to Kashmir a healthy man. This did not stop me from getting jobs though; I arrived at Heathrow and then caught the train to Bradford with my brother-in-law. He was very young, aged twenty-one years and it was his first experience of travel outside Pakistan. We were both on a train and it was heated, I had been on trains before but not one that had heat. We could not figure out where the heat was coming from at first, my brother in law asked *'Do you think the train is on fire'.* Eventually, we summed it up and reckoned because it was a cold country, the train must be heated.

Life in England was very tough for the first ten years or so until our communities became established. For those first few years, work was plentiful and many of us lived in small houses which were overcrowded. Some of us would sleep during the day whilst others worked and then we would work night shifts whilst others slept in the same beds. That is probably where we picked the label of being 'dirty'. The English people thought Asians were dirty. It was us that were struggling to get used to the new way of life. We were used to washing our bodies down with clean water, and here people were fortunate if they had a bathtub to wash in. I remember some of my relatives who lived in places like Bury in Greater Manchester having to share communal toilets with other people who lived on the same street; they used to have to take their toilet paper with them.

In the initial years here in the UK, food and the spices that we were used to were rarely available but we managed. We were lucky in Bradford as the first *roti* houses (takeaways that served curry and chapatti) opened around 1961 near where we lived on Little Horton Lane. But for others living in other parts of the UK, life was very different, they would have to make curry out of tinned vegetables and eat bread as a substitute to chapatti. Then as more people started to come over, more of our culture and cuisine became available.

In a timely entrepreneurial spirit, one of my cousins, along with other family members, opened *Halal* meat shops; one of the first ones in Bradford. There was one on Church Street, just off Heaton Road and another one which was on White Abbey Road. They also stocked the rice, flour, and spices that are part of our cuisine. By the late 1960s, many of us had been joined by families so our way of life changed to accommodate this.

Throughout the 1960s I worked (on and off) in places like Bolton, Lancashire, and Sedbergh on the outskirts of the Yorkshire Dales where I was the only brown-skinned person. I also worked as a weaver in a mill in Cowling and Denholme on the outskirts of Keighley and Bradford later in my working life as well as some mills in Bradford. Work was easy to find in those days, even though some mills had notices up saying 'No Blacks' there were plenty of jobs. You could leave one job in the morning and be hired again in the afternoon at another place. Work did not bother me as I was used to hard work. Although I could drive, I did not take the driving test here in England so I relied on buses to take me to places. Sometimes my journey could be more than two hours on the bus but that did not bother me either as lots of other people did this too.

However, my back had been giving me problems since arriving in the UK and the pain was getting worse, at first, the Doctors thought it was Lumbago but late in 1964, I was diagnosed with Pott's disease (T.B of the back). I was working in a mill in Worthington, near Manchester then. My back was operated on and I was in the hospital for a long time. Even though medical care was good then, the nursing sister who took my stitches out had taken them out too soon after surgery and it opened my wounds again. Regrettably, she was discharged from medical practice straight away once the doctor had seen this. I spent almost two and a half years in and out of hospitals as one operation led to another, my back; thighs and stomach were all operated on. The nurses would come and turn the plank that I was laid on every hour or so. My medication would be given to me and I would be washed and fed. I did not enjoy this, it was a sad and undignified existence as I was used to doing things for myself and not being reliant on others. As Muslims, we are taught to be humble and grateful for everything at all times. So even though my pride was shattered I was grateful that I was being looked after as my wife and family were far away in Kashmir.

I was back in Bradford by late 1965 and started to look for work. I had obtained a pet too, a black cat. I do not know how I got him, probably a stray but he just started to come around and then stayed. I remember he used to sleep in my bed near my feet at night. I had to go to the 'Dole Office' as they used to call it in those days to sign onto the on the unemployment register and show that I was looking for work. I did not notice but the cat had followed me there. When my turn came to sign on, the clerk or officer that was seeing to me said *'Is that your cat'?*

I turned around and looked and to my astonishment there he was stood beside my feet. I was worried for a bit, perhaps this was a government building where cats were not allowed? So not knowing what was going to happen next, I said *'Yes, but I am sorry I do not know how he got here'.*

The officer was perfectly fine about and added an extra

shilling to my allowance each week for the cat's food! I was taken aback, I did not expect this but that is one of the things I have always liked about this country that the state showed care for its citizens or at least it did in those days. I know some people would disagree with me but that is how it was then and how I experienced England.

I recovered from my illness around 1966 but realised 'the myth of return' – that I could not go back home. Even though as an ex-military person, my treatment would be free, however, healthcare such as that in England at the time would not be available in Pakistan. So as soon as I recovered, I started to work again and it was at this point that I sent a sponsor for my wife to join me. She joined me in 1967 and we lived in a house less than a mile outside the city centre. Initially, she found it difficult to adjust to the cloudy dark atmosphere of Bradford at the time. It was a different place compared to the sunny place of our origins. Most immigrants found it difficult to adjust but the men got out and about whereas the women from our community were stuck at home so it made it worse. We used to burn coal for heating and to warm the water which did not help as the soot from the coal everywhere. It had to be cleared from the fire each morning.

A few of our other relatives had brought their families over by then and we had a small family network. Overall there were still not that many families from our community who had settled here by then and it was a very male-dominated environment. My wife and other women would wash their clothes by hand during the week so that when the weekend came the washing lines were clear. This was so that the men living around our neighbourhoods would not know that these houses had families living in them. This was a protective precautionary measure which men of my generation took to guard our families against any kind of ill harm which would be seen as *baistey* (shameful).

I suppose the sentiment in those days was that since there were so many young males around often without families, they may be attracted to women of the same community. Although many of the young males had fun in other ways, they did not bother the women in their community. But those of us with families still had to be careful and protect our women. This was not because we did not trust our wives but because we could not trust others due to the circumstances of the time. Having said this, our culture is very family orientated and most men in our community generally tend to respect women, well at least my generation did. My wife found it difficult to adjust to this sort of life and called it '*metti kaid*' which means sweet imprisonment. In our home village we had a *Biradari* system and we did not have restrictions such as this. So the women did not need to be secluded as such and all of them – mothers, daughters, sisters, and wives were seen as the whole community's *izzat* (honour).

We all worked hard and on Saturday evening, the men would gather in one house and the women and small children in another. We would play cards and other games to occupy ourselves whilst the women cooked and got dressed up and did fun things for themselves. One of my cousins had a television, it was black and white and there were only about two channels then. We would take it in turns to gather at each other's houses but mainly the men gathered at my cousin's house and the women were at our house. Occasionally, the women would get a chance to go to the cinema with the rest of the family as we had one in Bradford that showed Asian films or to a *Meena Bazaar* (women's bazaar) where they could buy the loose material. In those days there were hardly any Asian clothes shop selling loose material which is what women in our community used to make up 'Shalwar Kameez' (traditional garments). Travel back home was not that frequent then as people could not afford to go regularly. So the women could not rely on their stocks being replenished from there either. My wife had a sewing machine, a big Singer machine that had a very heavy stand made out of cast iron. She managed to make her clothes and do alterations. A few of our cousins had machines too; one of them even had a knitting machine that she used to make jumpers and cardigans for her family.

We initially lived in a house on Forster Street, Lady Lane in Bradford (now part of the grounds of the University of Bradford). But by 1968, I had saved up enough money to put a deposit to buy our first house on St Michael's Road, just off White Abbey Road where we stayed for most of our life in this country. I bought the house with a friend for a sum of eight hundred and sixty pounds from Raymond's Bakers who owned the bakery shop on the corner and the bakery next door to us. The house that I bought was third from the corner, the baker's family had lived here. In those days, it was the only house in the neighbourhood that had an upstairs bathroom. Everyone else's toilets were outside in the backyard and baths were in the cellar. All the people that I spoke to about buying the house said that it was too expensive but I bought it anyway. I paid the baker two pounds per month until the late 1970s to pay off the rest of the loan. It was handy for me as the bakery and the baker's shop on the corner were still operating next door until the early 1980s.

My daughter, Amina or Aamnah as we have always called her at home was born on a Friday morning in September at the Bradford Royal Infirmary. In those days, men of my generation did not go into the labour ward; instead, I sat in the waiting room. Our cousin Zubaida, a colonel's daughter had a degree from Pakistan and was fluent in English; she was present at Aamnah's birth. God bless her she had two young children of her own to look after at the time. She cooked for nearly ten people twice a day as she was the only female in her family. She was caring and still managed to spare the time to attend antenatal appointments with my wife and be present at Aamnah's birth!

We were delighted to have a daughter but the doctors gave me the sad news that she may only live for a few hours. Like our other children, she was not a well-child. I named her quickly in honour of our prophet Muhammad's (peace be upon him) mother as I did not want her to die without a name.

I did not tell my wife what the doctors had told me but I knew shortly after our daughter had been born, and I recited the *Kalima* and *Istiqamah* (Islamic Oaths) in her ears that I had to go home and make arrangements. So I purchased a small coffin from a local undertaker, the *Kaffan* (Islamic Shroud) from a local Pakistani man who used to sell cloth door to door on a cart in my area at the time and put everything under the bed.

Thanks to Allah the Almighty, fortuitously our daughter survived and we brought her home two weeks after her birth. The family back home had written letters congratulating us and had suggested names but I had made up my mind and was going to stick with Aamnah. I forgot to tell my wife about the coffin until she accidentally discovered it whilst she was putting our daughter's things away under the bed. We used to have those sorts of beds in those days, they had metal bases with springs on the base and the space underneath the base of the bed was used as storage. She asked me 'what's this?' and I had to tell her what the doctors had said, she just wept.

I was in my early forties when Aamnah was born so I did things like taking her out in her pram to the town centre and the local neighbourhood. It probably looked a bit strange at the time as not many men were hands-on in their children's upbringing but I enjoyed taking her out. I became a bit of reclusive dad in later years though.

In those days a lot of people use to visit our house from other places as it was a family home; many were still without their families. One of our prominent visitors at the time was my second cousin Brigadier Rt. Raja Habib Ur Rehman (Lala Ji) who I have mentioned previously. He was visiting the UK and other European countries on an official visit in 1969 and stayed with us at St Michael's Road for several days, he was well received and lots of people came to visit him. He did not recognise me initially, probably because the last time we met was when I was a healthy young man in the military. But now that I had been ill and had several surgical operations, I had probably aged somewhat. He thought he was staying with some extended family members not knowing it was my wife and me (we were all related). He greeted me initially with all the others, and then after we had eaten, we sat down and started to talk. Inquisitively he asked me 'Are you Abdul Rehman'? I just laughed and said 'Yes, did you not recognise me'. He replied, 'No, I didn't.'

He then just got up out of the seat and gave me a huge hug which was befitting for cousins. I used to have a photograph of him and all of us cousins which was displayed on our living room fireplace for years; the photograph changed hands and is not available anymore.

People heard about his visit through the press and then word got around that he was staying with us in Bradford so they just flocked to see him. It was a very busy week for my wife and other women in the family due to all the cooking and serving of visitors. In our religion as Muslims, we are supposed to follow our Prophet Muhammad (peace be upon him) and his example known as a *Sunnah* and so we should serve our guests immediately without thinking about preparing elaborate meals (just serve what you have). But in our culture, it is considered disrespectful of the guest if you do not go out of your way to serve them with specially prepared food. Sometimes the guests can be curt and point out that no effort was made for them. So we often end up cooking extra and food that we would not cook on an everyday basis for our guests. The only thing in those days was that we did not have any of the readymade packaged food that became available in later years so everything had to be prepared and cooked from scratch and often in big quantities.

One of the neighbours, a man who lived a few doors away on the other side of our street had served with *Lala Ji* in the Far East. We were having our breakfast, he came to our back door, still in his pyjamas and dressing gown and his indoor slippers. He was not expecting a family to be living there; he thought it was just single men living there which the case was usually in those days. My wife stepped aside and moved to the back end of the kitchen when she saw this strange man entering our house. *Lala Ji* just got up and hugged him. The man that lived in our street was so excited to see him that as soon he heard he was here; he just rushed to our house without thinking to go to the front of the house. He later apologised to my wife and said that he did not mean to startle her. She was fine about it as she understood why he had done so. In later years we got to know the family well and become friends, so my wife knew his wife and daughter well and our daughter became friends with their granddaughters.

Chapter 10

TIME IN PAKISTAN

Nearly two years later after the birth of our daughter, we were blessed with another son, Jamil-Ur-Rehman. My wife was in the early stages of pregnancy and returned to Pakistan in February 1970 as she had lost her youngest brother; Muhammad Ajmal whom she was very close to. He had passed away just a few months after our daughter had been born. She took his death badly and was still grieving. She was not able to attend his wedding but changed into new garments each day for each ceremony as she would have done had she attended his wedding celebrations. He had only been married for about five months before his life was taken so quickly, he had been bitten by a piousness snake. Some months after Muhammad Ajmal's death she was given some more dreadful news which became unbearable for her. My wife's other brother; Muhammad Salim who was about four years older than her, had been serving in the army in East Pakistan (Bangladesh) but was discharged on medical grounds due to Tuberculosis. He was very seriously ill so she wanted to go to Pakistan to be with him and her family. Sadly Muhammad Salim died too some months later but at least she was there with her family.

I joined my family in Pakistan in 1972, we had a house there before we came to England, it had been resurrected and a new house had been built in its place. At the time, we still did not have an electricity supply to our part of the village (although the main central village of Panjeri did) but in anticipation, my wife and I had collected electrical appliances. We had taken an electric iron, kettle, fans, and electric blanket and gardening tools. As well as the electric stuff we had taken Danish made kitchen utensils which were kindly gifted to us by our cousin Abdul Hamid who worked in England and Denmark. We had purchased vases, ornaments, stainless steel cutlery, odd pieces, and a full set which was packaged in a silver-coated box and had blue velvet on the inside. In later years, some of the stuff was stolen including my father's rifle from my parent's house where it was being stored.

We hired builders to construct a water well in the garden which was situated at the end of the courtyard, just beside the front gate. So we know had our water supply in the house. The well had the old metal turbine wheel (before the days it was fitted with a motor) which used to bring water up from the well in the *Tindaan* (several metal containers). As the wheel spun around, the *Tindaan* would tip the water into the metal container that was laid across the top of the well. The water would then flow from the container into a large cemented basin which was called an 'Oluu'. The basin used to collect the water was sometimes closed so that the kids could play in the water. Our children and their cousins had a lot of fun when they were younger as having a well in the garden meant they spent hours turning the cog-like wooden handle that was attached to the spinning water wheel. They used to try and catch the water in their hands as it was coming to the top. Our daughter even snapped her wrist as a child because she did not pull her hand out in time out as the metal water wheel was spinning.

I had purchased the land adjacent to the house which meant it had a very big courtyard that was split into two. I have always loved gardening, so as soon the water well was completed; and now that there was water to feed the plants, the rest of the plot of land was made into a *bagh* (garden). I planted orange, lemon, *jamun* (plum like fruit), *shahtoot* (mulberry), and loquat trees. We had two traditional berry trees pronounced '*berri*', one was with the larger *pemdhi* berry and the other one was a much smaller tree called a '*cockni berri*' which produced small red berries. I also planted a *swangana* pronounced *swanjana* tree. It has a long drumstick type of green beans which are used to cook as a vegetable and pickled as *achar* (food preserved in oil). I also planted seasonal herbs and vegetables including coriander, onions, garlic, tomatoes, and potatoes. In another part of the *bagh* we grew barley, corn, and whey. We had traditional seeds in Pakistan that we planted but I had taken vegetable and herb seeds from England so they came in handy for the garden. Once the trees came of fruit-bearing age, all the relatives and extended family were given free subsidies each year – that is still the case.

In later years, the children found a mango plant growing on one of the village dumps (where people emptied their rubbish) whilst they were playing out in the fields and brought the plant home. They made a ditch deep enough for the roots and then planted it in the garden near the garden well; they watered it daily. No one expected the plant to grow but surprisingly it did! So with the help of one of their uncles, they managed to build a brick stand around the plant. This was to stop the wandering animals belonging to others in the village from eating it that came into our garden if the gate was left open. The plant had grown to about two metres high. Folklore has it that in the initial years, a mango tree usually needs the shade of a bigger tree to grow up to a certain height so that it can survive the hot sun. Then the shade of the bigger tree needs to be removed so that the mango tree can branch out. Unfortunately, the mango tree did not survive after my family came back to England, probably because it had not been watered properly. Otherwise, my family would have home-grown mangos to look forward to in the summer months.

We also had a family dog, named *'Kala'* (meaning black) simply because of his black colour. One of the children's maternal cousins brought two puppies, one in white and one in black, and allowed them to take one. Our children chose the black puppy and affectionately called him *'Kalu'*. If my wife ever went anywhere he would follow her behind and then come back when she had reached her destination. Once she visited some of my relatives in my mother's home village which is some distance away from our village, *Kalu* followed her there. She had not realised that he had followed her until she was at one of my relative's home. Everyone at my mother's village was surprised that he had done this but I suppose that is a dog for you – they are very loyal animals. He was given water and something to eat before he departed for his return journey home. He even followed the children to the village school gate each day, once they were inside, he would come back home. Every time we had been anywhere, he would be waiting at the gate, wagging his tail and sticking his tongue out. We always made sure there were water and food provision for him but he seemed to miss us. Sadly, after my family returned to England in the mid-1970s, *Kalu* was left with relatives and died shortly after. We were told he made some very disturbing noises which sounded like cries! Maybe he missed the kids or that was just the end of his life even though he was only about 8 years old.

Feuds over land are common in Pakistan, people who are second or third cousins can claim it when someone sells it. It is a bit farcical but that is the law over there and unwillingly I got embroiled in this too. The land that I purchased adjacent to my house was claimed by another relative of the family who sold it to me. This other person put a claim on it through the courts and we have been involved with a lengthy court case ever since which is never-ending. Some of my family are from the same lineage (through their father's side) as the other person, so they had a dispute over it too. I have ended up paying a very hefty price for this land and also the anger and frustration of a feud that I should not have been dragged into. I should have been cleverer and not taken people for face value; they had hidden agendas that a straight-minded simple person like me would never even think about. They settled their scores in devious and cunning ways with each other and threw the baggage on my lap. As if suffering all those illnesses in the 1960s was not enough, I ended up getting my head cut open by an axe! A member of the other family pierced into my head as they were feuding with the family that was related to me. I was there to stop them but instead became a victim of it all. The wound was deep on the top of my crown about the width of an axe and as soon as I got hit from behind, I just fell to the floor unconscious. I spent almost a considerable amount of time in *Bhimber Hospital* after this incident. I was bedridden and weak with the amount of blood I had lost. My wife nursed me at home for nearly a year after that.

The land is regarded as one of the sources of *fitna* (evil) in Islam, where people and nations feud over it, and for me and my family this purchase certainly was. I regretted buying this land as it brought nothing but misery even though I had no malice on my part, and did not do anything wrong. Since this had become a feud to settle scores and people were stooping to low levels. I was not going to back down either—after all, I had brought the land through honest means. The court case has been going on since then. The thing that let me down in my absence was that even though some members of my family were the cause of it, no one apart from a few people were prepared to go and integrally represent me wholeheartedly. They all had their vested interests. So the court case kept going on. My representation was passed from brothers to nephews and extended family. The other person could not take his anger out on those members of my family as they had outsmarted him by taking control of land that belonged to him so he kept venting his anger out at me and claiming my property. He even tried to get the land that my house is built on (purchased in the 1950s) onto his name! He was very clever too, he was able to offer *rishwat* (bribery), that is what they do in over there. They offer judges and lawyers sums of money and so they kept re-opening the case. In the end, I have ended up spending more on the court case than I did for the original land that I purchased. This has happened to so many others too, land or property that they have purchased by honest means has been deviously taken from them.

CHAPTER 11

BACK TO ENGLAND

I returned to England in 1974 and started to work in the mills as weaver again. My wife and children joined me in August 1976. Our daughter had been ill in Pakistan and it was life-threatening, she had been hospitalised there. Thankfully my mother-in-law did not agree to the doctors operating on her in Pakistan. She was admitted to a hospital and the doctors in Jhelum had diagnosed her with a burst appendix; if she had been operated on she would have almost certainly died! It was nothing to do with an appendix; she had developed another condition. Upon their return to England, I collected my family with my cousin, Abdul Khaliq from Heathrow Airport. Aamnah was ill – she was bending over as she came out of the arrivals section. I just picked her up and got her into the car and we drove up to Bradford.

On the evening of the second day after arriving here, we had to rush Aamnah to St Luke's Hospital in Bradford;

she was x-rayed on a big scanner and operated on more or straight away the next day. My wife and I were present at the hospital; we did not have access to a telephone at home so the family had to ring the hospital from a telephone call box several times in the day to enquire how she was. They had to wait until the evening to find out that the operation was successful and she was out of theatre safely. The surgeon that operated on her was an Indian doctor who spoke to us in Punjabi to tell us what they had done – he explained it as like having grass like roots in her stomach. It was a strange explanation which we interpreted as that there was some form of growth.

It was a tough time; our children were very close and had not been separated before. Our young son, Jamil was left at home, not yet going to school with his uncles and cousins; he missed his sister and mother. My wife and I spent most of the time in the hospital. Our daughter's condition was serious; she was on the children's ward but had been given a separate room overlooking the main ward. She did not speak any English and so her mother was allowed to stay with her during the day. It was Ramadan and my wife used to go to the hospital at around 9:00 am every day, I would finish my shift from Pennine Fibres in Denholme and go straight to the hospital at around 7:30 pm. My wife would go home to prepare for the opening of the fast; we had our cousin (who was also my wife's brother in law) and his sons living with us too at the time. I would stay at the hospital until around 9:00 pm, Aamnah would go off to sleep by then and it gave me just enough time to get home for the breaking of the fast or opening as we refer to it.

As Muslims we believe with every hardship, there is ease, – that is life. Nothing remains the same and so for us, things were alright for a few years. I did not have any more health issues and our daughter had recovered. Both our young children were settled in school, they had learned to speak English fluently within a few months after arriving back here in the UK. They both attended a specially designated language centre school for a few months (about four or five) and then were allocated places in mainstream schools. Our son started Green Lane Primary School in 1977 and our daughter went to a primary school in Heaton for a year and then started Manningham Middle in September of the following year.

Although we were not educated people, we were fairly liberal parents for our generation. My wife and I were cultured but we did not want to place too many restrictions on our children. So when Aamnah was selected to go on a school residential we allowed her to go despite the sceptical comments that were made about the trip being a mixed group of boys and girls. She was only around ten years old then and quite innocent so we did not want to start to impose these kinds of restrictions on her. Jamil was allowed to pursue karate classes even though we could not afford it. He was fond of cricket and football and he played in local teams which took him out and about. We did not have any transport to take him to matches so he made his way to places independently. They have both always appreciated this freedom.

We did not have a *Masjid* (mosque) near to our home at the time but my wife and I wanted to ensure the kids both learned the Quran properly so after they finished their initial learning from a lady who taught in the neighbourhood. They attended a Masjid which was about a mile away from home, they walked there and back. They got picked on by some other kids at the Masjid because they were not local enough but we ensured they completed their Quran before they left.

But then in the winter of 1979, the car we used to get home from work (Pennine Fibres, Denholme) broke down several times. It was snowing very heavily and I had to keep getting out of the car to wipe the snow from the windows. It was coming down so heavily that the wipers could not cope and keep up with it. I remember feeling not so well when I got home. My wife tried all the home remedies but nothing seemed to work. I went to see the doctor but my general practitioner was on holiday so I was seen by a locum who did not diagnose the condition correctly and gave me inadequate medication!

I had severe pain in my left eye and my skin had now erupted. I was ill at home for about a week before an ambulance was called; upon reaching hospital I was told it was Shingles. It could not be treated with heat near the eye area as it would have been if it had been on the body. The hospital staff tried to treat it but my sight in that eye had been affected and my skin around that area was permanently scarred. My memory had been affected too.

I was advised to make a complaint against my general practitioner. I had known him for some years and it was going to be an uncomfortable experience. One of my relatives and I spoke to him first and to my face, he was more than apologetic but afterward he thought I was crackers! Although he did not make the mistake, the locum doctor was someone he allowed to cover for himself – probably a relative. In the end, I decided not to pursue the complaint as nothing was going to come out of. The damage had already been done; nothing was going to rectify my sight and loss in memory. But fate has a way of showing itself. Some years later it emerged that my doctor himself was a fake! He was not properly qualified and had stolen another doctor's certification from Pakistan. He had been practising in this country for years. Nobody would have known any different until someone reported him and the testimony in the court of an observant pharmacist who had taken notes of the incorrect medications he had been prescribing to patients. It made me wonder whether the locum that was substituting for him was properly qualified or another one like him.

I had to give up work on ill-health grounds after this and never formally worked again. I was in my mid-fifties and not prepared to retire. It was a shock to the system and I found the first few years hard to cope with. Not having to get up for work and not providing for my family was not something that I felt comfortable with – it was not in my religion or culture. I did not want to rely on state benefits but at the time I did not have much choice in the matter.

I did reluctantly agree to my wife getting a part-time job as a seamstress in a clothing firm which was just around the corner. I think she wanted to do something and contribute to the family's income. Going out to work was not common in Pakistani women of her generation in those days, though a lot of them stitched garments at home for factories. To our relief, it turned out to be mostly women working there including the owner's wife and daughters. The family that owned the factory were people who came from the same part of Kashmir as we did.

We had obtained another black cat which started to come around in the late 1970s. Our children called it 'Bugzy'. My wife and I thought they were saying 'Bugthy' and we did not know what it meant. They had conjured up this name because of the state the cat was in when it started to come around, it looked like a stray cat and was in a bit of bad state. Bugzy was around for some years, even though people kept telling us not to keep a black cat for some reason, they called it *'nausat'* (bringing bad luck). My wife and I were not suspicious people, we knew what happened to us was written for us by Allah SWT and it was in our fate. So we kept Bugzy, we think it was a female from her face as she did not ever have kittens. She had probably knouted before she came to us. She was good at catching mice, we never had problems with mice considering we lived next door to a bakery but some of the neighbours did. So people used to borrow her if they wanted to get rid of the mice but they would always return her. A member of the extended family borrowed her because they had mice in the building where they were operating their business from but then passed her onto another person who was experiencing the same. We never got her back, our children often used to ask what happened to her but we did not have any answers for them.

Our children eventually grew up and got jobs, they both have a university education. This for my wife and me was worthwhile as our life ambition of having a better future for our children was almost complete. It did not matter that they got the jobs that paid lots of money but having an education and not going through the same hardships as we did is was what mattered. Even though I had served in the war with British soldiers, coming to the UK was still a culture shock. We did not have much of an education from our home country so coming to a new country where we did not know the system or speak the language fluently was difficult. Aamnah and Jamil did not have anyone to guide them as such. We are grateful to Allah SWT that they have stayed on the straight path and managed to complete their education and gain decent jobs. At least they will not have to do manual jobs in difficult settings because of their lack of English language.

The only things we taught our children were to be good Muslims first and foremost, hardworking, be humble, and honest. Allah will take care of the rest. We did not teach them too much about being Rajput either, it did not matter much; all that did was that we were good Muslims and decent people. We lived in a community with people of various backgrounds but everyone was close and almost like family. Our generation had left their loved ones behind so the people whom we lived near and worked with were our family now. My wife always said to the children that the neighbours were her *baradari* (clan) and her brothers and sisters. She taught the kids from an early age that blood relatives would not be there first in their time of need, so to accept the neighbours like family and be there for them too. Our relatives lived in all parts of the UK; there was hardly anyone here in Bradford so it took them time to get here. True to word, we experienced this several times such as family deaths, me becoming ill, and at general times of need. We had good neighbours who were like brothers and sisters and they would be the first ones there if anything happened.

There was a real sense of community in our neighbourhood; people looked out for each other. The back doors were never locked, anyone could come anytime but people were always polite and well-mannered to knock first before they entered the house. Since most of the men in the neighbourhood worked evenings as taxi drivers or in other settings, the women were free in the evenings. They used to stand outside their back gates and chat to each other whilst the kids played until as late as the day drew to a close. It has changed now in our community too with the younger generations as they have attained education and better jobs. So some of them have flown the family nest and as a result, people have become distant. The other thing that has happened is that each family's children have grown up and had families of their own. So within individual families, there are enough people to think about that they do not always have time for others.

We had some funny incidents too in those days. In our neighbourhood, apart from our house, most of the other households had toilets in the huts at the end of the back garden up until the late seventies. One of the families that lived opposite, their daughter came downstairs to find the lights on in the backroom and outside toilet so she got suspicious. Unknown to her the father had come from somewhere and went to use the outside toilet; he had switched the downstairs lights on. She did not think that another member of the family could have gone out to use the toilet instead she automatically thought they had burglars! She started to scream aloud and shout 'chor, chor' (burglars, burglars). The father who was still outside in the back garden thought the burglars were in the house. He was worried about his family so he started to shout 'chor chor' in the garden so that he could get attention and some help! We the neighbours heard the shouting and rushed out of our houses to their house. There was a lot of noise and confusion, the men checked their house and found no one inside. They asked the daughter where she saw them and what they looked like? She stated that she did not see anyone just that the outside lights were on and she had switched everything off before going upstairs. We had a bit of laugh afterward about the whole thing but that's how things were then – at least everyone came to their aid and stuck together.

Over the years, like all families, we had several funny incidents in the family too. By the 1980s most of the extended family had moved onto other places but still came to visit. Our nephews and nieces often came to Bradford for family visits and stayed with us, people in our communities did not use hotels then. On day one of my wife's nephews had purchased a copy of the Telegraph & Argus (T&A), our local newspaper, he was sat in our house drinking a cup of tea, suddenly he burst out laughing and the tea just came rushing out of his nose and mouth! We were all a bit startled as to why; we did not know why he was laughing hysterically whilst he was still choking. He started to speak when he got his breath back and said *'Look! What they've written about you'*?

He started to read the article to us, apparently the photographer at Belle Vue Studios on Manningham Lane that we all used to go to have our pictures taken had retired and passed his entire collection over to a local museum archive. The headline read *'Hi Mum! We're fine'* and the picture on the front page of the T&A to go with this article was of me, my cousins, and one of our nephews! Out of the thousands of pictures taken by this photographer over the years, they chose our picture. The article was not particularly complimentary either, it said that we (Asians) used to hire clothes, jewellery, and decorations to have our pictures taken to show our newfound wealth to those back home. The irony of it was that the old suit that I purchased in the 1960s was still hanging in the wardrobe in the bedroom. My nephew who also was featured in the paper was furious; he remembered how he had saved up to buy the suit he was wearing in the picture. He wanted to sue the paper for telling lies. He did not live in Bradford but had come up to visit us at the time of the picture. We had a laugh about it when they initial shock had worn off but decided not to do anything about approaching the paper as we saw it '*baistey*' (shameful) as more people would find out. None of our neighbours whom we had lived beside for years had recognised us; they all said that if we had not pointed it out to them, they would not know that it was us in the picture. So it was best to leave it alone. Ironically, my cousins and I were not wearing any borrowed jewellery as the paper stated.

The article in the T& A and the actual picture that was taken:

(Article Courtesy of Bradford Telegraph & Argus)

*My cousins, Abdul Khaliq Khan (bottom right),
Mohammad Afzal Khan (back left) and nephew Nasir
Ahmed (top right) with me (bottom left) (Photograph
Courtesy of Bradford Museums & Galleries)*

CHAPTER 12

THE CURRENT PRESENT

It is now spring of 2009; I am sat in an armchair in my living room back home in Bradford and relaying the story of the years I spent in the army to my daughter who seems to be interested in writing things down. She has written notes previously too. I am not a particularly lettered person so not sure why she wants to write things but I am alright to tell her some of it. The rest of it will stay with me as I do not wish to share all of it. Aamnah and Jamil are aware of a lot of it already – I used to tell them little stories when they were younger.

Life is strange and I have now come to accept that Allah SWT is the best of planners. Back in 2003, I went to Pakistan to be with my sister who was ill, little did I know that I would lose my wife suddenly in September of that year. As I have mentioned before she was a fair bit younger than me (about 12 years) and I had been the one who had been ill. She was generally well until her last few years. I always thought I would go first and she would outlast me but it was not meant to be that way.

She just suddenly became ill and passed away within two weeks. Her cancer did not show itself until the very end – we did not see it coming. I was left numb and in shock. She was younger than me, a rock-solid genuine woman with a strong faith but who was very humble and graceful. She had been a good wife and looked after me all these years. I never expected her to go before me, I was bewildered. Yes – selfishly, my old age was wrecked, what would happen now? I could not think past this. This was a total setback.

Thankfully Aamnah and Jamil were both at her bedside when she passed away in hospital in Islamabad. At first, she was admitted to Kharian Cantonment Hospital for nearly two weeks and was then sent home. My son came over as soon as he heard she was ill, she went into a coma for five days, and upon waking she was calling his name. Her last wish was granted as she wanted to be buried in our ancestral village.

I think the doctors had told my brother-in-law, Major Abdul Qayyum, that she did not have long to live but he did not say anything; he probably did not want to upset our children. They were both grown up so would be able to cope and maybe it would have prepared them for the shock too. So when Saeeda came home from the hospital, the house was full of visitors, our large hall was packed; every chair and *manjee* was taken. It was like that at the hospital too, she had a steady stream of visitors but being a military hospital the staff did not like it, so they kept telling people to leave her bedside. We could not say anything to the visitors as most of them came from distances to see her. In our culture and religion, it is customary to visit the sick and classed as a good deed.

Saeeda was home for a few days but then her condition deteriorated overnight and we arranged an ambulance to take her back to the hospital. It was night so I could not go but before she left, as a dutiful wife she asked me forgiveness if she had wronged me in any way (which she had not). I had asked her for forgiveness when her condition deteriorated in the hospital. As Muslims, we are supposed to ask for forgiveness regularly and in our culture, we do it often too, and especially a husband and wife at the time of death. We had a long marriage (almost fifty years) and most marriages are not without issues. The fact we survived for so long in the face of the trials, hardships, and the extra-familial issues that were imposed upon us was a blessing. I knew then that she knew she was not coming back home and I was just left feeling helpless.

She had been fairly well until the last few years of life. Some of it was health-related and some due to hurt caused by the actions of extended family. Although on the surface she showed grace but internally she took it badly, she was deeply hurt and worn out. My wife was a very strong character; she had enough pride and honour to be able to deal with it. She did not get involved with gossip, backbiting, and stoop down to the level of others but it was difficult and took its toll on her health.

Other than what was written our fate, much of stresses were due to years of inner family squabbles and difficult and broken marriages which caused hurt and anguish. People used certain others for selfish motives, it impacted all family members, family loyalties were tested and lead to broken family ties. In our culture marriages are not just between individuals but also unions of families. It is fine if these marriages within families work but if there are any issues, then whether they like it or not, the whole family gets dragged into it.

Even though we not part of the decision making, it was strange how events and decisions made amongst others nearly four thousand miles away could impact our lives here in the UK. Moreover, it was hurtful in how they manipulated the situation to get those who did not want to be involved to get dragged into it. Their behaviours and attitudes were despicable.

Then the gossip, bickering, backstabbing, lies, blame, stirring, and drama starts. Whilst every family has the peacemakers – those who try and hold things together.

However, every family has members who scornfully mock too. Although on the surface, they show care and compassion, they have feelings of Schadenfreude. Seeing others in turmoil or misery helps to satisfy their ego and settle old scores. They are like spectators who literally clap their hands in epicaricacy and secretly rejoice. I suppose their true colours show at times like this but it is what you can expect from people who lose their ghairat (honour and pride) for short-term selfish gains.

People can choose to protect themselves by totally cutting their ties with all the relatives involved but then that would go against the teachings of Islam as you cannot cut blood ties. Besides, why would people deny themselves and their children, the love and affection of all the good relations that exist for the sake of a few mischievous and roguish freaks? Instead, they can save themselves from becoming like the others and not get embroiled in the deceit and revenge games. It is better to turn the other cheek and walk away gracefully – that is having the upper-hand, they cannot control you.

So in February 2004, I returned to England with my daughter who had gone for an extended visit. My wife's passing had turned the tables; I could not live here in Pakistan whilst my children were in England. Though most of the extended family was around, it would not be the same. The *ronack* (charisma) that was around her was gone and nothing could replace it. I do not think I fully appreciated her or realise this in her lifetime but it hit me after her passing. I was never a man who showed too much of his emotions, perhaps that is the way I had been moulded from a child losing my father to becoming a soldier. But I think we had a good understanding of each other to know what the other was thinking and feeling without vocalising it too much. She certainly did, she could read my mind. After her death, I could not even look at her pictures for some time so I instructed my daughter to remove them.

A lot has happened in these last five or six years. I have been over to Pakistan once for a month but it is not a place for an old man like me who needs some help. My life is with my children and grandchildren and not with the extended family. I have come to the realisation that was my last visit, the next time I go over it will be a coffin. I have instructed my children that my final resting place should be my ancestral village too. I want to be buried there, next to my *Baba* (father). I am confident that they will obey and respect my final wishes.

Alhamdulillah (thanks to Allah) I think I am lucky and blessed at 84 years of age; despite all the illnesses and hardships, I have been all right. I am still very independent and do not need a lot of care. I have remained active and fairly agile up until now and my senses are all intact. I just have difficulty in hearing people. My mobility is slightly reduced due to Asthma and Chronic Obstructive Pulmonary Disorder. I have renal failure too partly due to taking medication for Hypertension for some years but other than that, on the whole, I am fairly well. The cancer is slow developing. I was shocked to hear that I had cancer at first but now I am not too fussed by it as we all have to go at some point. I would much prefer to go whilst I have all my senses and am not completely dependent on others.

My daughter has looked after me since my wife's death; she drives me to places so I get to go out and about with the family. I usually like to go to the town centre and the local shops. Aamnah usually drops me off on her way to work and I make my own back. The house is a bit of hill so it is getting difficult for me to go up the hill but I am fine coming down with the aid of my walking stick. On the weekend, I will go with the family to the shops, attend functions, visit extended family and friends; my family make time for me and even take me out to the restaurants when they eat out. I used to do this when I was younger with my cousins but have not done much in the last twenty years or so, it is nice to go and be included. Though I only see young people or people who are younger than me – no one of my age. It is sad that I do not see many people my age hardly anywhere, perhaps because a lot of them have passed away and others are not able to take themselves out. That is one of the reasons I did not want to go into a day-care centre when it was offered to me as I saw younger people who were classed as 'older'. I did not feel that I had that much in common with them. I tried a few times but did not feel comfortable so did not go again.

My grandchildren visit over the weekend, we usually eat together and I watch them play in the garden. My children work so evenings and weekends are the times they get together. Fortunately, we have a very strong community in England now and lots of services are available to us which did not exist when we first arrived here. Technology has moved on so much too, I have access to TV channels from Pakistan in my living room so I can get all the latest news within minutes. I still like to read the newspaper too. We all have access to phones and many people back in the village have phones too so we can speak to people regularly. A far cry from when used to have to write letters or send recorded taped messages on cassette recorders and wait for weeks or months for a reply.

The other family that I have are our neighbours. There is an old Arab proverb that says something to the effect of 'do not look at the house but look at the neighbours' when you are buying or moving to a new place. Thankfully we have always been blessed with good neighbours. Our first home was amongst good people and they were like our brothers and sisters. We live in a different area now and our neighbours are all mainly young people but nice families. It is generally a quiet street with lovely views overlooking the hills. Our immediate neighbours originate from the same part of Azad Kashmir as we do so we have become very close. Hina or 'Sheena' as she is affectionately known and her children are like our adopted daughter and grandchildren. She was very close to my wife and then after her passing, she has kept an eye out for me too. She is like my second daughter, around when Aamnah is not. I know that I can rely on her.

I have always been a keen cook; I learnt to cook in the army and then perfected it more when I came to England as my wife was not around then. Even when I was younger I did not want to bother my mother so I could make my tea. In those days we cooked using outdoors using wood. I started to do more cooking when I had to stop working here in England. My wife started to work so I would usually make the *handi* (curry) and she would come home and sort the rest out. These days, much to my dislike my daughter is cautious and does not let me cook unless she is in the kitchen with me; she will hover around and watch over my shoulder. We seem to at conflict with this, to my anguish it seems she has taken over the kitchen. This had become my department over the last twenty years or so and something I did not want to give up. To my embarrassment, I have on a few occasions not turned the gas cooker off properly in the recent past few years and burnt the curry so she has reason to be extra careful. I still get involved by cutting the vegetables, onions, and garlic. I like to stir the *handi* when she is making it too – just habit but I suppose it makes me feel like I have contributed.

As Muslims, our neighbours have rights over us like similar to the rights of blood ties so we have practices of sharing food with neighbours. So we get to taste each other's culinary skills too. We pass a dish over to our neighbours when we cook some of my favourite recipes such as *Shalgam Khosht* (meat with turnips) *Keema Karelay* (bitter gaud and mincemeat), *Keema Matar* (mince with peas) *Paya* (hooves), *Sarsoon Ka Saag* (spinach), *Ghost Pillau* (rice with meat) or something like *Karri Pakoray* (yoghurt based curry with onion baji) and any sweet dishes.

I enjoy watching TV, especially the news, comedy (our family favourites were Laurel and Hardy), programmes about nature and wildlife, films involving the army, athletics, and wrestling which I used to go and watch in person especially when Big Daddy and Giant Haystacks came to St George's Hall in Bradford.

I also like to watch programmes about the military and the Allied Forces Commemorations of the D Day landings and other victories. I was not a hero by any means but it saddens me that our part, the roles that the soldiers from the Indian Sub-Continent and those from other Commonwealth countries played are hardly ever mentioned. Some of them were real heroes – at least their contributions should have been remembered. There were hundreds of thousands of us who served alongside the British and other Allied Soldiers in both the World Wars and other battles. We fought alongside them and made lots of sacrifices too but we do not seem to be included in the commemorations or the celebrations as I thought we would be. It would have been good if our services and sacrifices would have been acknowledged and remembered too. I wonder why? Did we not matter? Are we any less as people? Were our lives not that important? Or were we just used to fulfil a need at the time? Although I have never been a bitter man or ever harboured any jealousy or resentment towards others, this saddens me. I am certain my comrades who have fought in these wars feel the same. In fact, they have told me so when we have spoken about things in the past.

I have noticed more recently the Ghurkhas have been featured in some of the parades which are pleasing to see. It is great to see British servicemen and women on parade with their medals – it shows they have pride. My medals have always been kept in a trinket box and my kit has been stored in one of the metal trunks in the house in Kashmir. I have never worn my medals or been pictured or paraded with them since leaving the army. So that is where they shall remain.

The army taught me lots of valuable skills too; I could darn my socks and put a thread to a needle if I needed to mend any clothes or to stitch buttons back on to shirts and much more. These were good skills as it meant not having to rely on others to do this if I needed to especially when I came to England.

In the summer I sit in the garden and watch the plants and flowers grow that my son-in-law plants. He is a keen gardener and a real handyman too. He was in the navy in Pakistan before he came to the UK, so as an ex-army man I can talk to him a lot about things. His life story is similar to mine in some aspects as he left home at seventeen years old to join the navy to do something to better his family's circumstances. He has made a lot of sacrifices for them which he is as proud of as I was for my family. By the grace of Allah, his efforts have been reaped and his family is now much more financially stable than they were twenty years or so when he left home.

The family adopted another kitten in 2007, it is a very pretty looking ginger and white cat that started to come around. She had a silver collar originally but eventually, it disappeared. We were not sure if the owner had released it or whether she had got rid of herself. My daughter heard someone in the street shouting '*Sousa or Souza*' so that is what she called the cat – *Souza* or *Suzy* as she is affectionately known. Souza is a really good cat, she has only littered in the house a few times and each time it has been in the winter when she has not been out. She is adored by my grandchildren and extended family members too, she is a very friendly cat. Whenever we have someone around, she circles around their feet and wags her tail as if she wants to be stroked.

My daughter brushes her regularly so her coat is nice and fresh looking. Like the other cats we have had, she sleeps at my feet too. She used to follow me to the top of my road when I went out independently. One time she even followed me to the bus stop on the main road which I had to cross to get the bus to the town centre. I was about to get on the bus and realised she was stood behind me so I picked her up and brought her back home. She and the TV is my companions during the day when everyone is out and about.

A few years ago my daughter and son-in-law had gone on a short break. Souza, she did not come home for nearly a week, so I was worried about her. When my daughter and son-in-law returned home I told them that Souza had not been home since they left and they started to look for her. They asked the neighbours but no one had seen her for a few days. Then a day or so later she came back in a rather skinny and poorly state. One of the neighbours had opened his garage and she must have gone in but then got locked in when he closed the door. He went back to the garage after nearly a week and when he opened the door, he heard her meowing. We were all a bit shocked and surprised too as it was in May and the weather had been nice. So for her to survive for that long without water was a miracle!

My hope for the future is that our communities will continue to thrive here in the UK and other countries but also be able to be good Muslims first and serve humanity. I hope my children and grandchildren will be a part of this and be able to conduct themselves with grace and honour. I hope they will be able to develop amicable solutions to keep the ties of brethren and kinship amongst relatives and community here in this country and with those in the country of our origin. If anyone can learn from any part of experience to better themselves and their families I will pleased.

Duas and Wasalaam

With my family and my brother.